THE PACIFIC WAY

Regional Cooperation in the South Pacific

MICHAEL HAAS

PRAEGER

New York
Westport, Connecticut
London

Library of Congress Cataloging-in-Publication Data

Haas, Michael, 1938–
    The Pacific way : regional cooperation in the South Pacific /
Michael Haas.
        p. cm.
    Bibliography: p.
    Includes index.
    ISBN 0–275–93121–8 (alk. paper)
    1. Oceania—Politics and government. 2. Oceania—Foreign
relations. 3. Oceania—Economic integration. I. Title.
DU28.35.H33 1989
327.9—dc19   88–27515

Library of Congress Catalog Card Number: 88–27515
ISBN: 0–275–93121–8

First published in 1989

Praeger Publishers, One Madison Avenue, New York, NY   10010
A division of Greenwood Press, Inc.

Printed in the United States of America

The paper used in this book complies with the
Permanent Paper Standard issued by the National
Information Standards Organization (Z39.48–1984).

10 9 8 7 6 5 4 3 2 1

CONTENTS

TABLES AND FIGURES

Tables

Figures

ABBREVIATIONS

AALCC	Asian-African Legal Consultative Committee
AARRO	Afro-Asian Rural Reconstruction Organization
ACC	Asian Coconut Community
ACP	African-Caribbean-Pacific Group (of EEC)
ACT	Australian Capital Territory
ADB	Asian Development Bank
AFP	Australian Federal Police
ANZAC	Australia-New Zealand Agreement
ANZUS	Security Treaty Between Australia, New Zealand, and the United States
APCC	Asian and Pacific Coconut Community
APPU	Asian-Pacific Postal Union
APPU	Asian-Pacific Parliamentarians' Union
ASA	Association of Southeast Asia
ASCA	Association for Science Cooperation in Asia
ASEAN	Association of South East Asian Nations
AsianRe	Asian Reinsurance Corporation
ASPA	Association of South Pacific Airlines
ASPAC	Asian and Pacific Council
A$	Australian dollar
C$	Canadian dollar
CALM	Conference of Asian Labor Ministers
CAPLM	Conference of Asian and Pacific Labor Ministers

CINPAC	U.S. Commander-in-Chief Pacific
CRIA	Committee on Regional Institutional Arrangements
CATV	Commonwealth Air Transport Council
CCOP	Committee for Co-ordination of Joint Prospecting for Mineral Resources in Asian Offshore Areas (of ESCAP)
CCOP/SOPAC	Committee for Co-ordination of Joint Prospecting for Mineral Resources in South Pacific Offshore Areas
CCPASWPR	Conference of Commissioners of Police of Australasia and South West Pacific Region
CERTA	Closer Economic Relations Trade Agreement
CFTC	Commonwealth Fund for Technical Co-operation
CGRA	Committee of Representatives of Governments and Administrations (of SPC)
CIRDAP	Centre on Integrated Rural Development for Asia and the Pacific
CPPS	Permanent Commission of the South Pacific
CRO	cumulative rules of origin
CULSOCEN	Cultural and Social Center for the Asian and Pacific Region
DAMA	demand assignment multiple access
DGCA	Informal Meeting of the Directors General of Civil Aviation, Asia and the Pacific
DWFN	distant-water fishing nation
EC	European Community
ECAFE	Economic Commission for Asia and the Far East
ECDC	economic cooperation among developing countries
ECU	European currency unit
EDF	European Development Fund
EEC	European Economic Community
ESCAP	Economic and Social Commission for Asia and the Pacific
FAO	Food and Agriculture Organization of the United Nations
FFA	Forum Fisheries Agency Secretariat
FFC	Forum Fisheries Committee
FFTC	Food and Fertilizer Technology Center for the Asian and Pacific Region
FIC	Forum island country
FLNKS	Kanak Socialist National Liberation Front

FVB	Fiji Visitor's Bureau
HIBAL	High-Altitude Balloon Atmospheric Sampling
ICAO	International Civil Aviation Organization
IGCC	Regional Organization for Inter-governmental Co-operation and Co-ordination in Family and Population Planning in Southeast Asia
ILO	International Labor Organization
INPFC	International North Pacific Fisheries Commission
IOC	International Oceanographic Commission (of UNESCO)
IPR	Institute of Pacific Relations
ITU	International Telecommunications Union
JSS	Cook Islands/Niue/New Zealand Joint Shipping Service
MSG	Melanesian Spearhead Group
NAFTA	New Zealand-Australia Free Trade Agreement
NASA	U.S. National Aeronautics and Space Administration
NIEO	New International Economic Order
NZ$	New Zealand dollar
OPEC	Organization of Petroleum-Exporting Countries
OTCI	Overseas Telecommunications Commission International Limited
PACOM	Pacific-Asian Congress of Municipalities
PATA	Pacific Area Travel Association
PATRCA	Papua New Guinea/Australia Trade and Commercial Relations Agreement
PBDC	Pacific Basin Development Commission
PEP	Pacific Energy Programme
PF	Pacific francs
PFDF	Pacific Fisheries Development Foundation
PFL	Pacific Forum Line
PIC	Pacific Islands Conference
PIDC	Pacific Islands Development Commission
PIDP	Pacific Islands Development Program
PILOM	Pacific Island Law Officers Meeting
PINS	Pacific Islands News Service
PIPA	Pacific Islands Producers' Association
PITDC	Pacific Islands Tourism Development Council
PNG$	Papua New Guinea kina

PPC	Policy Planning Committee (of Pacific Islands Conference)
PRAS	Pacific Regional Advisory Services
PRTDP	Pacific Regional Tourism Development Programme
PSA	Pacific Science Association
PTDF	Pacific Tuna Development Foundation
RCT	Regional Committee on Trade
RRDP	Regional Research and Development Programme (of SPFFA)
SAARC	South Asian Association for Regional Cooperation
SC	Standing Committee (of Pacific Islands Conference)
SCONZ	Shipping Corporation of New Zealand
SEAFDEC	Southeast Asian Fisheries Development Center
SEAMEO	Southeast Asian Ministers of Education Organization
SEANZA	Central Banks of Southeast Asia, Australia, and New Zealand
SEATO	South-East Asia Treaty Organization
SGATAR	Study Group for Asian Tax Administration and Research
SIGNIT	signals intelligence
SI$	Solomon Islands dollar
SP CANGO	Committee for Air Navigation and Ground Organisation (of SPATC)
SP COMET	South Pacific Committee of Meteorologists (of SPATC)
SP FINCO	Finance Committee (of SPATC)
SPARTECA	South Pacific Regional Trade and Economic Co-operation Agreement
SPATC	South Pacific Air Transport Council
SPBEA	South Pacific Board for Educational Assessment
SPC	South Pacific Commission
SPEC	South Pacific Bureau for Economic Co-operation
SPECTEL	South Pacific Regional Meeting on Telecommunications
SPFFA	South Pacific Forum Fisheries Agency
SPHS	South Pacific Health Service
SPICIN	South Pacific Islands Criminal Intelligence Network (of CSPCP)

SPJC	South Pacific Judicial Conference
SPMDP	South Pacific Maritime Development Programme
SPOCC	South Pacific Organisations Co-ordinating Committee
SPRCAC	South Pacific Regional Civil Aviation Council
SPREP	South Pacific Regional Environmental Programme
SPRSC	South Pacific Regional Shipping Council
SPTC	South Pacific Trade Commission
SPTDP	South Pacific Telecommunications Development Programme (of SPECTEL)
STAR	Joint CCOP/SOPAC-IOC Working Group on South Pacific Tectonics and Resources
STAS	Short Term Advisory Services (of SPEC)
TAG	Technical Advisory Group (of CCOP/SOPAC)
TCCC	Taxation and Customs Cooperation Conference
TCSP	Tourism Council of the South Pacific
Techsec	Technical Secretariat (of CCOP/SOPAC)
TRANET	Transit Navigational Satellite
TRM	Tripartite Review Meeting (of CCOP/SOPAC)
U.K.	United Kingdom
UN	United Nations
UNCTC	United Nations Center for Transnational Corporations
UNDP	United Nations Development Program
UNESCO	United Nations Educational, Scientific, and Cultural Organization
UPNG	University of Papua New Guinea
U.S.	United States
USAID	United States Agency for International Development
USP	University of the South Pacific
US$	United States dollar
WHO	World Health Organization
WS$	Western Samoan tala

PREFACE

For approximately the last two decades, I have focused my attention on regional intergovernmental organizations. This volume examines South Pacific regional cooperation, though my previous efforts have concentrated on Asia.

There are several reasons for my expansion in focus. Many of the Asian organizations that I visited in 1971 had, by 1978, increased their membership to include the island nations of the South Pacific, some of which had only recently emerged as independent states. By 1985, the year of my third extended field trip to the region, a few of the older Asian organizations had changed their names to include "Pacific" in their titles. Accordingly, I decided to visit countries of the South Pacific to gain insight into the perspectives of countries that were already playing a role in regional cooperation, which was once exclusively Asian. In the process I uncovered a much larger number of South Pacific regional organizations than I had anticipated.

A brief explanation of the basic concepts is in order. As before, there is some difficulty in defining the scope of what is to be covered. Initially, I had hoped to write about intergovernmental organizations with head-quarters in an Asian country and membership limited to a minimum of three Asian countries, outside the framework of the United Nations system or other international organizations headquartered elsewhere. However, several key organizations had no headquarters at all—the Association of the South East Asian Nations (ASEAN) and the Asian and Pacific Council (ASPAC) in particular. I therefore modified my definition of "organizations" to include intergovernmental cooperative arrangements outside the UN system with regular meetings, at least three sovereign countries considered to be members, and a special name to label the organization.

For the South Pacific, the major definitional dilemma is whether to include organizations with some nonsovereign member countries. Again, I applied the rule that at least three independent countries are needed for an organization to be truly intergovernmental. Application of this rule produces the paradox that some organizations, such as the Conference of Chiefs of Police of Australasia and the South West Pacific (CCPASWP), existed long before a third independent member country first participated.

The rule that no truly regional organization can be a suborgan of an organization headquartered elsewhere is needed in order to exclude Commonwealth and UN organizations. Thus, as soon as the Committee for Co-ordination of Joint Prospecting for Mineral Resources in South Pacific Offshore Areas (CCOP/SOPAC) became independent of the UN's Economic and Social Commission for Asia and the Pacific, it became possible to include CCOP/SOPAC in this volume. At the same time, the South Pacific Air Transport Council (SPATC) was formally subsidiary to the Commonwealth Air Transport Council (CATV), though in actuality SPATC operated quite autonomously of CATC. Thus, I have been careful not to be too legalistic in my criteria of inclusion and exclusion.

Finally, I define the "South Pacific" to include the island nations from the Pitcairn Islands on the east to Palau and Papua New Guinea on the west, from Micronesia on the north to Australia and New Zealand on the south. As Honolulu is the headquarters for several intergovernmental organizations, including nations from this geographic area, I had no alternative but to include Hawaii within the scope of "South Pacific" as well. The Permanent Commission of the South Pacific (CPPS), headquartered in Lima and composed of four Pacific countries in South America, is excluded, as is the Vancouver-based International North Pacific Fisheries Commission (INPFC).

There are a number of conventions peculiar to a volume based in large part on interviews and perusals of documents that are not generally available to the public. One is that my sources are not directly identified, protecting confidentiality. A second peculiarity is that references for each organization are cited together at the beginning of each section; the reader should realize that few are available in a public library, even in the South Pacific. The most complete storehouse of materials is in the Pacific Collection, Hamilton Library, University of Hawaii. A third convention is that I refer to U.S. dollars unless otherwise indicated; other currencies are converted into U.S. dollars. A fourth practice is the use of dotted lines in organization charts to refer to defunct organs.

At this point, I would like to acknowledge assistance in my efforts to compile the materials on the South Pacific. The list is rather long, as I received considerable cooperation wherever I went. For the South Pacific Health Service, I wish to thank Elizabeth Crowley, Marion Thompson, and H. B. Turbott. For the South Pacific Air Transport Council, Neville Potter, Judith Robertson, Terry Russell, W. Tucker, and Damien Wallace. For the South Pacific Commission, Kevin Earl, Michael Eastgate, Bess Flores, Richard Herr, and Tiu Livino. For ANZUS, Richard Baker, Desmond Ball, Helen Clark, Brian Lockstone, Andy Mack, Col. Robert Martin, Michael Ovington, and Capt. A.J.L. Tyrrell. For the Conference of Chiefs of Police of Australia and the South-West Pacific Region, Ann Sue, D. M. Weeks, and Marie Wilson. For the Conference of South Pacific Chiefs of Police, Joe Franklin and Steve Rusbatch. For the South Pacific Judicial Conference, M. Fox, Robert Hefner, Samuel P. King, Thomas W. Murphy, Sir William Prentice, A. Seru, and M. D. Scott. For the Pacific Island Law Officers Meeting, John Flower, E. Murray Heddrick, Leo Keke, and Neromi Slade. For the University of the South Pacific, Ron Crocombe, Philip Rama, E. C. Reade, and G. D. Singh, Seona Smiles, and Esekia Solofa. For the South Pacific Board of Educational Assessment, Trevor Rees. For the Cook Islands/Niue/New Zealand Joint Shipping Service, Denise Almao and Vince McBride. For the Pacific-Asian Congress of Municipalities, Galen Fox and the late Victor Givan. For the Pacific Islands Tourism Development Council, Chuck Gee, Andrew Gerakas, Jerry Norris, and Martin Pray. For the Pacific Islands Conference, Te 'o Fairbain and Charles Lepani. For the South Pacific Labour Ministers Conference, M. Twigg and S. C. Cornwell. For the Committee for Coordination of Joint Prospecting for Mineral Resources in Offshore South Pacific Areas, Jim Eade, Joiji Kotobolavu, and Alonzo Cruz Matos. For the Tourism Council of the South Pacific, Malakai Gucake and John Yacoumis.

Concerning the South Pacific Forum, several individuals provided assistance: Peni Drodrolagi, Witi Ihimaera, Leo Keke, Malcolm Leader, Peter Moore, Henry Naisali, Simeon Raiwai, Mahe Tuponuia, and Rene Wilson. For information on the Pacific Forum Line, which has quasi-independence from the Forum, I am grateful for assistance from Ormond Eyre, George Fulcher, W. J. MacLennan, Max Olson, and D. West. With respect to the subsidiary bodies of SPEC, special mention should be made of the following: Regional Committee on Trade and SPARTECA, R. E. Jennings, James Makasiale, Dennis Miller, John Nicolson, Sam Osifelo, Adam Robertson, John Stephens, Karai Vuibau, and Helen Wong; South Pacific Forum Fisheries Agency, Judith Swan and Roniti Teiwaki; South Pacific Regional Civil Aviation Council, Arnold Van Buuren; South Pacific Regional Shipping Council, Paul

McDonnell; South Pacific Regional Telecommunications Meeting, P. Lynn Holloway and E. James Wilkinson; South Pacific Trade Commission, William McCabe.

Several others deserve mention for assistance of a general nature. These are Robert Benzinger, Rakai Catalina, William Fisher, Greg Fry, Jill Hutchison, B. P. Johnston, Nicholas Lorimer, Rajendra Kumar, Carlyle Thayer, and Atilya Williams.

As always, there are inevitable changes in organizations and personnel between the time that research is conducted and a book is published; organizations change, members come and go, and budget windfalls and shortages cannot be anticipated. What is important is the theory of the "Pacific Way" as the basis for cooperation in the region.

Michael Haas
Honolulu

FOREWORD

Most observers believe that the "Pacific hemisphere" consists of Canada, China, Japan, parts of Southeast Asia, the United States, and possibly Australia and New Zealand. The idea of a "Pacific community," as espoused by officials in New York and Washington, has united the industrial countries in the region with countries of the Association of South East Asian Nations (Brunei, Indonesia, Malaysia, Philippines, Singapore, and Thailand) in a larger partnership.

Yet these countries are at the rim of a hemisphere; their governments tend to treat the Pacific as only one arena of international concern. For the island nations of the South Pacific, the Pacific is everything— a source of natural resources, a path for transportation, and a gateway for intruders. Indeed, Pacific island peoples were colonized and largely neglected over the past two centuries, leaving them among the poorest of the poor countries in the world today.

As Pacific island countries became independent, they began to develop a form of joint international solidarity known as the "Pacific Way." Through this solidarity, a variety of regional organizations has arisen in the South Pacific. The agenda of these organizations is to build consensus, develop a common front in international affairs, and gain external assistance to be less, rather than more, dependent upon the outside world.

The Pacific Way did not arise in an instant. Regional cooperation in the South Pacific was virtually a monopoly of colonial powers until the 1970s, when the South Pacific Forum was established. The Forum, in turn, shifted the agenda of prior regional organizations while starting new ones to function in such fields as fishing zones, telecommunications, trade, and transportation.

The record of regional cooperation in the South Pacific, though not widely known outside the region, has changed the terms of diplomacy for the island nations. Officials in Paris and Washington, operating in the region as they do without much empathy for nor an understanding of the Pacific Way, are losing influence as a result.

This book defines the Pacific Way, sketches some of the important details of regional cooperation in the South Pacific, and addresses issues concerning prospects for integration of South Pacific regional organizations into a single coherent structure. In addition, the book demonstrates that the Pacific Way is a new form of international interaction—a refreshing contribution to theories of regional integration.

Readers of the book not only will obtain a greater understanding of the South Pacific and its future, but also will learn that the culture of the Pacific Way is a force that cannot be taken for granted. The power of the Pacific Way is decidedly spiritual. The beauty of the South Pacific, often revealed in exotic travel posters, is to be found within its peoples, as this volume is proud to assert. The world would indeed be a better place if all countries were to adopt the Pacific Way as a basis for international diplomacy. This book takes a small step in advancing that viewpoint.

1   *THE PACIFIC WAY*

INTERNATIONAL HISTORY OF THE PACIFIC

Some 2,500 or more years ago, ambitious migrations of seafaring peoples began to spread from the periphery of Asia to remote archipelagos in the Pacific. The International history of the South Pacific is one of limited state relations until the late eighteenth century, when imperialist countries colonized the region and gained control of resources and markets. Few efforts to establish centralized rule over the South Pacific are recorded, as the vast distances between the archipelagos precluded all but modest and limited systems of communication (Figure 1.1).

CONCEPT OF THE PACIFIC WAY

Despite geographic diversity, the peoples of the South Pacific islands nevertheless share a common culture in regard to international relations. One aspect of "culture" is the set of shared beliefs and sentiments that serve to orient leaders of states to their roles as international actors.[1] The similar roles of leaders of South Pacific island states reflect shared cultural orientations regarding their similar histories of precolonial, colonial, and postcolonial development.

The reason for this convergence, as argued herein, is that historical conditions shaped a common interest in peaceful modes of state behavior. Interlopers from outside the region further underscored the virtues of peaceful statecraft, and the destiny of countries of Asia and the Pacific has come to depend more and more upon efforts to forge a common identity and a compatible operational code in foreign policy.

Figure 1.1
Map of South Pacific[a]

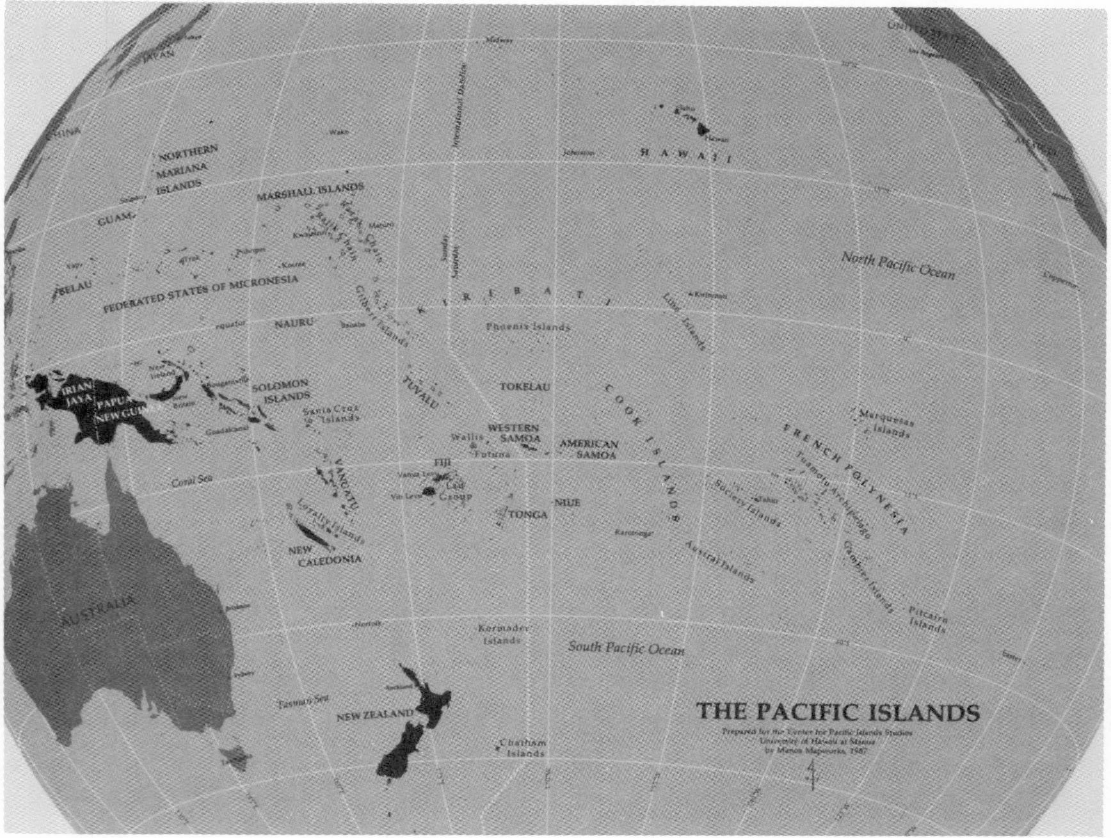

2

Figure 1.1 Continued

Entity	Capital (Island)	Political Status
American Samoa	Pago Pago (Tutuila)	US unorganized, unincorporated territory
Australia	Australian Capital Terri-tory	Independent state
Cook Islands	Avarua (Rarotonga)	Self-governing in free association with New Zealand
Federated States of Micronesia	Kolonia (Ponape)	Self-governing in free association with USA
Fiji	Suva (Viti Levu)	Independent state
French Polynesia	Papeete (Tahiti)	French overseas territory
Guam	Agana (Guam)	U.S. organized, unincorporated territory
Hawaii	Honolulu (Oahu)	U.S. state
Kiribati	Bairiki (Tarawa)	Independent state
Marshall Islands	Majuro (Majuro)	Self-governing in free association with USA
Nauru	Yaren (Nauru)	Independent state
New Caledonia	Noumea (New Caledonia)	French overseas territory
New Zealand	Wellington (North Island)	Independent state
Niue	Alofi (Niue)	Self-governing in free association with New Zealand
Northern Mariana Islands	Saipan (Saipan)	U.S. Commonwealth
Palau (Belau)	Oreor (Koror)	Self-governing in free association with USA[c]
Papua New Guinea	Port Moresby (New Guinea)	Independent state
Pitcairn Islands	Adamstown (Pitcairn)	U.K. colony
Solomon Islands	Honiara (Guadacanal)	Independent state
Tokelau	admin. from New Zealand	New Zealand territory
Tonga	Nuku'alofa (Tongatapu)	Independent state
Tuvalu	Fongafale (Funafuti)	Independent state
Vanuatu	Port Vila (Efate)[b]	Independent state
Wallis and Futuna	Mata-Utu (Uvea)	French overseas territory
Western Samoa	Apia (Upolu)	Independent state

[a]Permission from the State of Hawaii to reprint the map. This inset has been modified, primarily to reflect changes since the map was first printed.
[b]Administrative center.
[c]UN Trusteeship has not yet been terminated.

3

The purpose of this chapter, accordingly, is to document the existence of the "Pacific Way" and to specify its content and associated determining conditions in regard to international relations.

Three major themes are developed. First, norms of international statecraft in the history of Pacific island politics are described. Second, the breakup of these norms and the resulting dependence on outside forces with the advent of Western imperialism are discussed. Third, the emergence of the Pacific Way in recent decades is delineated as a method of liberation from outside influences through the development of a common identity.

TRADITIONAL PRACTICES OF PACIFIC ISLANDERS

Since the peoples of the South Pacific were sparsely settled on thousands of islands over vast areas and separated by rough seas, they did not develop complex bureaucratic systems of rule. Systems of education, literacy, and philosophy did not develop on a formal basis. Therefore, the content of the root cultures of the many Pacific island peoples is not to be found in authoritative texts by indigenous writers. Great emphasis was placed on oral history. Practices of the islanders were recorded by the earliest visitors with considerable care. While Melanesian society valued personal skills somewhat more than hereditary bases for leadership, Polynesian society was divided into commoners and various levels of chieftanship, with the wisdom of the ruling chiefs well respected throughout an island.[2] Religious traditions were observed strictly, and religious leaders had a symbiotic existence alongside secular leaders. War was a method for determining the extent of a chief's domain, but it was regulated by specific codes of conduct.[3] For example, war was in daytime, with the place and time agreed upon. No war took place during certain times of the year, and a truce could be declared at any time during battle. Once war started, it was pursued with ferocity; the vanquished were slaughtered unless they were successful in pleading to live as slaves of the victorious chiefs. Tonga was the only kingdom believed to be successful to any degree in subduing the other peoples of Polynesia. Defeated peoples are often thought to have escaped to new islands to the west. Population pressure and scarce resources also accounted for continuing migration until the extremities of the Pacific were ultimately reached.

Though Melanesians were more inclined to fight to defend their societies, what was most impressive to the Westerners who first arrived in Polynesia was the friendliness of the people.[4] For centuries, the Pacific islanders treated themselves and others with extraordinary courtesy and kindness at an individual level—a spirit called *aloha* in

Hawaii, with similar meanings and spellings in other Pacific languages. Subsistence agriculture and fishing accustomed the people to a sense of community in which every individual felt obligated to assist everyone else to ensure mutual survival and happiness. The common people did not challenge the ruling class. However, the nobility of one island might be jealous of the plenty of an adjacent island, and war could then occur, with commoners immediately obligated to fight for their chiefs. Thus, the commoners did not compete among themselves; this was a luxury afforded to the ruling chiefs. Land had a sacred character. Property rights were maintained in a complex, integrated hierarchy; the rights of individuals, while clearly recognized, were subsumed by the ruling chiefs, who were considered to have dominion over land as a trust on behalf of all people. The ideal leader gave food, which could not be preserved for any length of time, and material gifts to all; this hospitality and sharing not only conferred prestige upon the giver, but also affirmed the common destiny of all members of the group.

The practice of talking out social problems, with all interested parties present, remains the primary method of conflict resolution among Pacific islanders when matters of rank and status are not relevant. "Unanimous compromise" is the ideal outcome; that is, some are expected when possible to endure personal sacrifice so that the community as a whole will have harmony.[5]

WESTERN INTRUSION INTO THE SOUTH PACIFIC

After the Roman Empire ceased to hold the Western world together, an unimpressive collection of warring feudal states arose in Europe. Europeans wanted some of the costly and exotic goods produced in Asia, but trading ships were not allowed to pass through Arab territories during the Middle Ages. New trade routes were discovered by explorers in the fifteenth century, thanks to advances in the technology of shipbuilding and seamanship, and trade increased as Europe went through a transformation to a capitalist economic system. In order to ensure the regular flow of commerce, European states first established ports in Asia along the trade routes. In due course New Guinea was first visited in 1526, Fiji in 1643, Tahiti in 1767, and Hawaii in 1778.

Free trade, however, was not allowed. Trading companies wanted exclusive access, and they called upon their governments to establish colonial control over territories adjacent to their outposts. Their ambitions to occupy larger territories required military force. Colonialism eventually carved up the territories of most of Asia and the Pacific. Fiji chiefs invited the British to afford protection in 1874. Great Britain established control over Papua, Germany over Northern New Guinea in 1884, and the Solomon Islands fell under British control in 1893.

Although France claimed the Society Islands as early as 1768, they were not annexed until 1881, and French Polynesia was not grouped into a single colonial entity until 1903. Hawaii was annexed by the United States in 1898, and in 1900 Germany and the United States divided Samoa into two parts and the British established a nominal protectorate over Tonga.

In some cases imperial rule was more heavy-handed than others. Christian missionaries accompanied the colonial administrators and were extremely successful in the Pacific Islands.

The political effects of colonial rule on the peoples of the South Pacific were many. Subsistence agriculture was transformed into export-oriented industry, making the peoples economically dependent. The local populations received limited benefits, if any, and lost a sense of control over their own destinies.

During World War II, the military forces of Imperial Japan demonstrated the weakness of Western colonial powers in Asia and the Pacific. Although Japan tried to justify its superpower role through such slogans as "Asian solutions to Asian problems" and "Greater East Asia Co-Prosperity Sphere" as early as the 1920s, Pacific island countries were not particularly eager to exchange European domination for Japanese direction. As a result, nationalist movements gained considerable support in Asia during World War II. When Western countries tried to reestablish control in 1945, their legitimacy had already been called into question, and the cost of continued imperialism was perceived as excessive to many politicians in the metropolitan countries. Institutional independence was the inevitable result, with some countries attaining their sovereignty sooner and more peacefully than others (Table 1.1).

Political independence did not bring economic independence. Colonial governors were withdrawn, but corporations with head offices in metropolitan countries remained. As the interests of corporations were entrenched before political independence, the economies of what were to be called "developing countries" were vertically integrated into a world capitalist system in which Pacific island countries exported raw materials at unfavorable terms of trade. History provided two models for economic development: capitalist prosperity through a long period of economic ups and downs and the Soviet Union's remarkable success in modernizing quickly through state direction of the economy in just 40 years. The victory of the forces of Mao Tse-tung in China by 1949 ightened capitalist countries in Asia—both the imperial powers that still maintained anachronistic control over various enclaves and territories and the newly independent states that had indigenous pro-Communist insurgents. The result was increased bilateral aid, the development of programs of multilateral economic assistance through

Table 1.1
Countries of the South Pacific

Current Name of Country	Previous Name (if any)	Previous Metropoles
American Samoa	Samoa	United States[d]
Australia		United Kingdom
Cook Islands		New Zealand
Federated States of Micronesia	Trust Territory of the Pacific Islands	United States (UN Trusteeship)[a,b,c]
Fiji		United Kingdom
French Polynesia	Tahiti	France
Guam		United States[c]
Hawaii		United States
Kiribati	Gilbert Islands	United Kingdom
Marshall Islands	Trust Territory of the Pacific Islands	United States (UN Trusteeship)[a,b,c]
Nauru	Naoero	Australia[a]
New Caledonia		France
New Zealand	Aotearoa	United Kingdom
Niue		New Zealand
Northern Mariana Islands	Trust Territory of the Pacific Islands	United States (UN Trusteeship)[a,b,c]
Palau	Trust Territory of the Pacific Islands	United States (UN Trusteeship)[a,b,c]
Papua New Guinea		Australia[a]
Pitcairn Islands		United Kingdom
Solomon Islands	British Solomon Islands	United Kingdom
Tokelau	Tokelau Islands	New Zealand
Tonga		United Kingdom
Tuvalu	Ellice Islands	United Kingdom
Vanuatu	New Hebrides	France & United Kingdom
Wallis and Futuna	Wallace and Futuna Islands	France
Western Samoa	Samoa	New Zealand[a]

[a]Former colony of Germany.
[b]Former colony of Japan.
[c]Former colony of Spain.
[d]Formerly an incorporated territory.

various United Nations agencies, and a projection of the cold war philosophy to the South Pacific.

Institutionally, the UN Economic Commission for Asia and the Far East (ECAFE) in Bangkok, known as "the economic parliament of

Asia,"[6] began to formulate ambitious plans for economic development. Commonwealth countries formed the Colombo Plan for Economic Development in South and South-east Asia as a non-UN conduit for aid to the region in 1950, and the Security Treaty Between Australia, New Zealand, and the United States, known as ANZUS, started in 1952. However, the states of the South Pacific were not immediately included in the scope of these efforts on their behalf; they were still colonies. By the time ECAFE became the Economic and Social Commission for Asia and the Pacific in 1974 and the Colombo Plan was retitled as the Colombo Plan for Economic and Social Development in Asia and the Pacific in 1977, South Pacific island nations had become even more dependent upon Western funds, Western technology, and Western priorities for the region. The focus of discussion in these bodies was on how much aid the outside powers were willing to supply, so the real aspirations of many Pacific island countries remained unstated.

THE PACIFIC WAY EXPLAINED

While the world was convulsed with conflicts associated with independence from imperialism after World War II, the island states of the South Pacific were considered to be far from both the cold war and so-called "preconditions" for achieving political independence. Although decolonization remained the trend, its attainment was perceived to be less urgent in the South Pacific. Plans to provide better education, health, and other benefits proceeded in the colonies of Australia, Great Britain, France, New Zealand, and the United States, but the pace was slow, and demands from the indigenous populations were hardly strident.

Immediately after World War II, efforts at regional cooperation in the South Pacific focused on the needs of outside powers. The South Pacific Health Service (SPHS) began operation in 1946 to provide medical personnel to Fiji and other countries of the region in part so that tourists from abroad could vacation without fear of contracting devastating tropical diseases. Of course, the primary beneficiaries of SPHS were the peoples of the South Pacific, but their role in decision making was negligible. The South Pacific Air Transport Council (SPATC) was set up in 1946, primarily to facilitate civilian air transportation across the Pacific from Australia and New Zealand to North America; the construction and maintenance of airport facilities at Nadi, Fiji, enjoyed high priority. Non-Fijians ran the Nadi airport, though Fijians performed some of the maintenance work. Elements of paternalism were present, and independence was thought to be a long way off.

By the mid-1960s many South Pacific islanders had been educated to run their own affairs of state. The bureaucracies of colonial administrations were staffed with a fair share of well-trained indigenous civil servants, though expatriates remained very much in control. New Zealand decided to grant Western Samoa full independence in 1962. Fiji became fully soverign in 1970, Papua New Guinea in 1975, and most of the remaining colonies raised their own flags in the 1980s. As local officials gradually assumed control of various functions at Nadi airport and health facilities, SPHS and SPATC, two of the earliest regional organizations set up by the colonial powers, were phased out (in 1969 and 1979, respectively).

In the context of the eventual attainment of independence in the South Pacific, Fiji's Ratu Sir Kamisese Mara, longtime Prime Minister, began to give a series of addresses concerning the Pacific Way based in part on the views of Ratu Lala Sakuna, who struggled for Fijian independence until his death in 1958.[7] The arena in which Mara found Western powers particularly insensitive was not a UN organ. Instead, it was the South Pacific Commission (SPC), set up in 1947 before the UN had established regional economic commissions. SPC had undertaken a wide variety of economic, social, and technical projects in the beginning, but countries of the region were not initially represented on the plenary body of the organization. Instead, a conference of the territorial administrations was to be held triennially to comment on SPC work, more or less after the fact. At the 1965 South Pacific Conference, Mara startled fellow indigenous leaders, as well as delegates from external powers, by proposing that the work programs of SPC should be formulated by countries of the region first, leaving the colonial governments in the role merely of ratifying and funding what had been approved by those destined to benefit from the various projects. In due course Mara's proposal became reality; the South Pacific Conference became the plenary organ of SPC, and the organ (known as the Commission) composed solely of colonial governments was abolished in 1973. In 1970 he presented the term in an address to the UN General Assembly. Then the launching of the South Pacific Forum, composed initially of independent countries of the region (thus excluding France and its colonies), provided the Pacific Way with a clear institutional home by 1971. At the same time, leaders from Australia and New Zealand, who felt a special responsibility for the island states of the South Pacific, have been included as equal partners in international cooperation in the region.

The Pacific Way was politically motivated—aimed at urging indigenous leaders trained outside the region to unlearn Western modes of conflict resolution. The Pacific Way, hence, is not a contribution to the field of anthropology but rather a reconstruction of practices believed to have existed in the past. The Pacific Way has called for increased regional cooperation in which the aspirations of South Pacific countries are to be at the core, while external powers are to keep their own ambitions for the region very much to themselves. The content of the Pacific Way, aptly called "a rather non-specific thing" by New Zealand Prime Minister Wallace Rowling in 1974,[8] has served as a symbol to unite diverse peoples into an awareness of unity and common destiny. However, latent rivalry between the island leaders has been articulated in the phrase "Melanesian Way" as a response to the fact that the Pacific Way concept was advanced by Fiji and *Fa'a Pasifika* by Western Samoa.

Perhaps more importantly, regional cooperation for the peoples of the South Pacific is an urgent matter; the countries lack basic resources. South Pacific regional cooperation affects the destiny of nearly all persons, so results must be practical and realistic.

We must therefore comment on each of the points of the Pacific Way. Since some observers claim that there is a difference between the Pacific Way and the style of diplomacy followed in the West, our comparison should help to identify important distinctions.

Pacific Solutions to Pacific Problems

The concept of Pacific solutions to Pacific problems is at the core of the Pacific Way. We can see this in a number of fascinating instances. For example, each country rotates in responsibility as host for meetings of many regional organizations; rather than uniform recordkeeping at the meetings (which would tax the clerical resources of many smaller nations), each host does what it can to provide secretariat functions. A second example is premised on the fact that the only natural resources of many small island nations are bananas, coconuts, fish, and, of course, the people. Aid projects have stressed increased productivity or diversified processing of existing resources—all to no avail in economic terms for a population so small and isolated that even the success of an aid project would make a negligible impact on the prosperity of the country. Accordingly, based on the experience of phosphate-rich Nauru, an idea arose that some of the South Pacific ministates should receive a cash contribution of, say, $10 million, to be deposited in a bank; indeed, Tuvalu now lives on the interest of such deposits. The cost to donor countries is greatly reduced, as all the bookkeeping, airfare, and personnel costs of various projects from now until the next century and beyond are to be saved, and the economic survival of particular countries is assured in an instant. A "Pacific solution" seems reasonable to countries lacking any important natural resources, and Tuvalu has now succeeded in having such a trust fund established through a consortium of offshore banks with financing from Australia and New Zealand.

Equality of Cultures

"The spirit of the Pacific Way," according to Tekoti Rotan, is "that dialog and discussion in an atmosphere of tolerance and goodwill offers the best prospects for the settlement of... differences...."[9] Meetings of South Pacific islanders, so long isolated from one another, are viewed in part as adventures in learning how similar are the attitudes and customs of the participants. The term "brother" is applied widely to reflect social reality more than biology, implying an ideology of mutual help, common origins, and thus common interests; the Hawaiian term *ohana* is often used to refer to the sense of community in which the extended family is broadly defined. As Ratu Sakuna once said, "Strive for the things that unite rather than those that divide."[10] Although Australia is the largest donor country in the region, and its delegates can be extremely verbal, the tenor of mutual respect within the dialog of the island nations has caused Canberra to play a constructive "big brother" role, and the island states have ruled out suggestions in some quarters that Australia and New Zealand should be consigned to observer status in such organizations as the Pacific Island Law Officers Meeting (PILOM). The peoples of the South Pacific show few signs of hostility toward their former colonial overseers, though there is a common realization that the native population was too often forgotten.

Unanimous Compromise

Under the Pacific concept of "unanimous compromise," a term coined in 1975 by Cook Islands' Prime Minister Sir Albert Henry, it is expected that "nobody gets left out."[11] Discussion often begins with modest comments by representatives of island nations, who seek outside assistance but feel too humble to make special pleas. Nonetheless, frank disagreements are articulated without causing resentment. Humility and appeals to emotion during discussions among island leaders have cultivated a kind of "give" (rather than the Western "give and take"). The South Pacific has been out of the mainstream of twentieth century technology for so long that the "give" involves the metropolitan powers: development assistance can be seen as a form of affirmative action, yet South Pacific leaders show profuse gratitude rather than exhibit a bitter mood of justice denied. Since warm interpersonal relations are highly valued, developed through intimate contact, informality also is a part of any meeting in the South Pacific, where Western business suits are almost unknown. Indeed, national dress is worn more often in the South Pacific than in many other parts of the world, reminding nonisland countries that the region takes pride in its pre- and postcolonial identity. Pacific islanders devote much effort to ceremonial gatherings; this is done in order to indulge the strong impulse to sociability.

Primacy of Political Goals

Political will prevails over practical considerations of administrative feasibility in the Pacific as well. The Pacific Forum Line (PFL), for example, was formed in 1978 to provide regular shipping to islands that had been neglected and abandoned; there was a hope of turning a profit but no solid evidence that a subsidy would ever disappear from the time when PFL was approved. Nevertheless, under new management in the mid-1980s, PFL appears destined to be a profit-making multilateral enterprise. The South Pacific Forum has consistently adopted resolutions asking France to stop nuclear weapons tests and to grant independence to its colonies in the region. Yet it was Australia and New Zealand, not the island states of the South Pacific, which took the nuclear testing issue to the World Court. When national priorities preclude a regional solution, nevertheless, countries are willing to accept political realities without rancor.

Pan-Pacific Spirit

Collective priorities prevail over national self-interest in the South Pacific. This is because regional cooperation from Western Samoa to Papua New Guinea is not just a means for building solidarity but instead an imperative for economic development. The Pan-Pacific spirit has served to focus attention on common needs and away from internal squabbling. Micronesian states emerging from lengthy U.S. trusteeships have been eager to partake of the spirit by applying for membership in a variety of South Pacific regional organizations. Maori Kiki has stated that joint responsibility and sharing of wealth are Pacific-wide characteristics.[12] He was doubtless thinking of the practice of affluent family members sharing their homes and meals with less affluent family members, a practice that applies as well to the obligations of village leaders toward commoners. Current efforts to provide regular telephone and television service, which might be expected to go to the most populous countries (Fiji and Papua New Guinea), were instead negotiated with communication satellite corporations on a group basis. The all-or-nothing approach pointed to the volume of business for all island nations and resulted in a comprehensive agreement in 1988 for the region, which was followed up by supplying and servicing ground stations for even Niue, the smallest island nation.

Optimistic Incrementalism

To some observers, "Europeans and Asians are regarded as being too serious," as the Pacific Way is considered by Asesela Ravuvu to be "the ad hoc way."[13] The tendency not to plan, to let the future take care of itself, may indeed be in sharp contrast with Western fastidiousness in planning and implementation. Pacific islanders are seldom pessimistic; they expect everything to work out in time. It is their patience and cheerful regard for the inevitability of amelioration that becomes a kind of self-fulfilling prophecy encouraging outsiders to be even more generous and helpful. The early thrust of the Pacific Energy Programme (PEP), which began in 1983, was on importing biomass and solar technology to increase energy supply; but when the sophisticated technology broke down, with no one available to be trained to repair or to maintain the equipment, the project may have seemed a boondoggle for foreign manufacturers to dump unwanted machinery in far-off islands. PEP instead realized that the entire project was too ambitious, abandoned the inappropriate technological solution in 1986, and energy conservation is now the focus of its attention. We could call this an instance of capitulation to the impossibility of progress, but a more perceptive view would be to say that a practical solution won out.

Each of the above six principles, in sum, reverses an axiom that might be used to describe how Westerners handle public policy matters. The Pacific Way arose as efforts were taken to cope with international problems of states that achieved political but not economic independence after World War II. Having found that Anglo-European methods can abet even further conflict in many instances, the Pacific Way emerged as an amalgam of the root cultures of the South Pacific, adapted to modern times. These principles, to be sure, are not alien to Western societies. But the Pacific Way is more likely to be a model of performance in South Pacific island public as well as private life, which those in the West endeavor to keep as separate realms.

SOUTH PACIFIC REGIONAL ORGANIZATIONS

Altogether, about two dozen regional organizations have been formed among countries of the South Pacific (Table 1.2). There have been at least four sources of leadership over the years.

Leadership of Australia and New Zealand

Australia and New Zealand were instrumental in the formation of the earliest South Pacific regional organizations. The South Pacific

Table 1.2
Formation of South Pacific Regional Organizations and Terminations

Initial Year as Regional Body	Name of Organization and Acronym	Year Ended or Suspended
1946	South Pacific Air Transport Council (SPATC)	1979
1946	South Pacific Health Service (SPHS)	1969
1947[a]	Conference of Commissioners of Police of Austra- lasia and South West Pacific Region (CCPASWPR)	
1948	South Pacific Commission (SPC)	
1952	Security Treaty Between Australia, New Zealand, and the United States (ANZUS)	1986
1968	Pacific Islands Producers' Association (PIPA)	1974
1970	Conference of South Pacific Chiefs of Police (CSPCP)	
1970	University of the South Pacific (USP)	
1971	Pacific-Asian Congress of Municipalities (PACOM)	
1971	South Pacific Forum	
1972[b]	South Pacific Bureau for Economic Co-operation (SPEC); South Pacific Forum Secretariat in 1988	
1972	South Pacific Judicial Conference (SPJC)	
1973	South Pacific Labour Ministers Conference (SPLMC)	
1973[b]	South Pacific Regional Telecommunications Meet- ing (SPECTEL)	
1975	Cook Islands/Niue/New Zealand Joint Shipping Service (JSS)	
1975[b]	South Pacific Regional Shipping Council (SPRSC)	
1976	Pacific Islands Tourism Development Council (PITDC)	1979
1976[b]	South Pacific Regional Civil Aviation Council (SPRCAC)	
1978[b]	Pacific Forum Line (PFL)	
1979[b]	South Pacific Forum Fisheries Agency (SPFFA)	
1980	Pacific Islands Conference (PIC)	
1981	Pacific Island Law Officers Meeting (PILOM)	
1981[b]	Regional Committee on Trade (RCT)	
1981	South Pacific Board for Educational Assessment (SPBEA)	
1983	Tourism Council of the South Pacific (TCSP)	
1984[a]	Committee for Co-ordination of Joint Prospecting for Mineral Resources in South Pacific Offshore Areas (CCOP/SOPAC)	
1986	Melanesian Spearhead Group (MSG)	
Totals	27-5=22 organizations	

[a]Began earlier as a nonregional body.
[b]Subsidiary body of the South Pacific Forum.

Health Service began in 1946 largely through New Zealand initiatives. The South Pacific Air Transport Council started in 1946 as a joint Australia-New Zealand-United Kingdom project. But by 1969 SPHS was phased out, and the work of SPATC was considered to be at an end in 1979. Colonial powers formed the South Pacific Commission in 1947; this was at a time when the United Nations was forming regional economic commissions, and the countries of the region could not wait for the UN to act on behalf of the region, so when the UN Economic Commission for Asia and the Far East (ECAFE) was formed, also in

1947, the South Pacific was largely outside its scope in order to avoid duplication of effort. SPC, in turn, set up a number of subsidiary organs, one of which arranged for the formation of an independent regional body, the South Pacific Board for Educational Assessment (SPBEA), in 1981.

Australian initiatives were primarily responsible for the Security Treaty Between Australia, New Zealand, and the United States, known as ANZUS. Australia's condition for signing the Japanese Peace Treaty in 1951 was that the United States form a regional security pact among the three countries, and its wish was granted when ANZUS emerged in 1952.

Australia and New Zealand also pioneered in regional organizations concerned with the administration of justice. The Conference of Commissioners of Police of Australasia and South West Pacific Region (CCPASWPR) began in 1903 as a body primarily composed of police chiefs from the various states of Australia; but by 1939 New Zealand had joined, and by 1947 Fiji began to attend, making the body more than a purely bilateral body.

New Zealand and the United Kingdom arranged for the establishment of the University of the South Pacific (USP), chartered in 1970. Australia, meanwhile, had founded a strictly national University of Papua New Guinea in 1965.

In 1975 New Zealand formed the Cook Islands/Niue/New Zealand Shipping Service (JSS) with two self-governing countries in the region whose defense and foreign affairs are still handled by Wellington. JSS continues to exist today.

Pacific Islands Leadership

Leadership from the island nations of the South Pacific eventually superseded efforts of the so-called "metropolitan powers." In 1968 Fiji, Tonga, and Western Samoa agreed to a Pacific Islands Producers' Secretariat for the Pacific Islands Producers' Association (PIPA) in 1968. Success of PIPA led Fiji and newly independent countries of the South Pacific to establish the highly successful South Pacific Forum in 1971. The Forum, in turn, sprouted many subsidiary bodies, including the South Pacific Bureau for Economic Co-operation (SPEC) in 1972 (whereupon PIPA was phased out in 1974), South Pacific Regional Meeting on Telecommunications (SPECTEL) in 1973, South Pacific Regional Shipping Council (SPRSC) in 1975, South Pacific Regional Civil Aviation Council (SPRCAC) in 1976, Pacific Forum Line (PFL) in 1978, South Pacific Forum Fisheries Agency (SPFFA) and the South Pacific Trade Commission (SPTC) in 1979, and the Regional Committee on Trade (RCT) in 1981.

In 1970 the first Conference of South Pacific Chiefs of Police (CSPCP) was convened by Fiji. In 1972 chief justices of the two Samoas convened the first in a series of South Pacific Judicial Conference (SPJC) meetings. In 1982 legislators from nonindependent Micronesia formed the Association of Pacific Island Legislatures (APIL); when former Trust Territory of the Pacific Islands countries become fully independent, this will be yet another intergovernmental body. Various subregional tourism councils at the nongovernmental international level were attempted in the late 1970s, but to no avail. The governments of the region decided to pool resources in 1983, forming the Tourism Council of the South Pacific (TCSP).

Leadership of Hawaii

Various groups in the State of Hawaii attempted to exert some leadership as well. The Pacific-Asian Congress of Municipalities (PACOM) started in 1971 as a project of the Mayor of Honolulu. The Governor of Hawaii launched the Pacific Islands Tourism Development Council (PITDC) in 1976, but it had ceased to operate by 1979 and was formally terminated in 1982. The East-West Center, a nongovernmental international organization, set up the Pacific Islands Conference (PIC) in 1980.

UN Leadership

United Nations organs were responsible for some South Pacific regional organizations as well. The International Labor Organization (ILO) served as a catalyst for the formation of the South Pacific Labour Ministers' Conference (SPLMC) in 1973, though Australia took a leading role as well. The Committee for Co-ordination of Joint Prospecting for Mineral Resources in South Pacific Offshore Areas (CCOP/SOPAC) began as a subsidiary body of ECAFE in 1972, but it became independent of the UN system in 1984.

This proliferation of organizations, to be discussed in succeeding chapters, has led to some concern for the establishment of a rationalized "single regional organization." The final chapter of the book discusses the omnipresence of the South Pacific Commission and the South Pacific Forum, conflict between them, the desirability and feasibility of a merger, as well as the larger significance of regional cooperation in the South Pacific today.

CONCLUSION

The Pacific Way has established itself as a norm of diplomacy. It provides unity toward the outside as well as a sense of cultural affinity despite a history that has many disjunctions. In the South Pacific, where the key issue is the survival of ministates in a world of overwhelming outside influences, the Pacific Way has pointed toward economic progress by focusing on imperialist neglect as a wrong that needs to be corrected. The principles of relevant solutions to local problems, equal treatment, consensus building through nonconflictual discussion, subordination of administration to politics, collective self-help, and informal incrementalism are means to an end. Their application varies somewhat, depending on circumstances and traditions, but the essence of Pacific island culture is that poor countries seek prosperity and dignity through a diplomatic style from which other parts of the world have much to learn. Indeed, the intended result is to place outside powers in a somewhat defensive position. The Pacific Way has established a dialog on how former imperialist powers can most effectively provide the peoples of the region with the diplomatic equivalent of reparations for past exploitation and neglect.

In the calm Pacific it is as if the suggestions of conflict theorist Georg Simmel[14] have been taken to heart: poor countries have surfaced a certain amount of hitherto latent conflict in their relations with their former colonial rulers in order to achieve a more integrated, harmonious solution. In the final chapter of this volume, the concept of the "Pacific Way" will be incorporated into the framework of theories of international integration, which place both conflict and cooperation into perspective in a larger theory of world community. That South Pacific countries prefer cooperative strategies is significant. Peace is seen as the normal condition of international relations.

The theory of the Pacific Way has been presented in this chapter. We now turn to the practice of the Pacific Way by tracing the development of regional cooperation among governments in the South Pacific.

NOTES

1. Lucian W. Pye, "Introduction: Political Culture and Political Development," in *Political Culture and Political Development*, eds. Pye and Sidney Verba (Princeton: Princeton University Press, 1965), p. 8.

2. Patrick Kirch, *The Evolution of the Polynesian Chiefdoms* (Cambridge: Cambridge University Press, 1984); Marie de Lepervance, "Social Structure," in *Anthropology in Papua New Guinea*, ed. Ian Hogbin (Melbourne: Melbourne University Press, 1973), pp. 1–60; Oliver Wyndette, *Islands of Destiny* (Tokyo: Tuttle, 1968), pp. 1–15. I have not attempted to discuss the experiences of Micronesia, as these peoples have only recently become independent and thus have not had sufficient opportunity to have an input into what I describe as the Pacific Way in this essay.

3. Kenneth P. Emory, "Warfare," in *Ancient Hawaiian Civilization* (Tokyo:

Tuttle, 1965), Ch. 22; L. L. Langness, "Traditional Political Organization," in *Anthropology in Papua New Guinea,* ed. Hogbin (Melbourne: Melbourne University Press, 1973) pp. 142–73.

4. Anne Chowning, *An Introduction to the Peoples and Cultures of Melanesia* (Menlo Park, Calif.: Cummings, 1977); Gavan Daws, *Shoal of Time* (New York: Macmillan, 1968), Ch. 1; K. R. Howe, *Where the Waves Fall* (Honolulu: University of Hawaii Press, 1984), Ch. 13.

5. *Auckland Star*, January 11, 1975, p. 1.

6. David Wightman, *Toward Economic Cooperation in Asia* (New Haven: Yale University Press, 1953).

7. Ratu Sir Kamisese Mara, *Selected Speeches* (Suva: Government Press, 1977).

8. Ronald G. Crocombe, *The Pacific Way* (Suva: Lotu Pasifika Productions, 1976), p. 4.

9. Crocombe, *The Pacific Way*, p. 15.

10. Stuart Inder, "Leaders and Their Legacies," *Pacific Islands Monthly* LVIII (December, 1987): 27.

11. Crocombe, *The Pacific Way*, p. 20.

12. Crocombe, *The Pacific Way*, p. 24.

13. Crocombe, *The Pacific Way*.

14. Georg Simmel, *Conflict and the Web of Group-Affiliations* (New York: Free Press, 1955); Louis Coser, *The Functions of Social Conflict* (New York: Free Press, 1956).

2   *TWO COLONIAL ORGANIZATIONS OBSOLESCE*

INTRODUCTION

When World War II ended, the colonial powers did not expect the peoples of the South Pacific to be able to govern themselves without tutelage from metropolitan countries. The reestablishment of trade and tourism in the region had higher priority, but there was a shortage of capital, facilities, and trained personnel of all sorts. Movement about the region required air transport facilities, and travel to the island archipelagos would be hampered as long as endemic diseases remained unchecked and untreated. Since a multicountry effort was required, the South Pacific Health Service (SPHS) and the South Pacific Transport Council (SPATC) emerged. By 1969 and 1979, respectively, both organizations had accomplished their aims and were terminated.

SOUTH PACIFIC HEALTH SERVICE[1]

When the balance of power during World War II in the Pacific shifted in favor of the Allied Powers, postwar planning for the British colonies proceeded. In the fields of medicine and public health, Fiji already had the Central Medical School with non-Fiji students since 1928, the Leper Hospital that had been accepting patients from outside Fiji since 1927, and the Nurses Training School that had been providing services to the following: American Samoa, Australia with respect to Nauru, New Zealand with respect to Western Samoa, and Great Britain's western Pacific colonies. After the war the Western Pacific High Commission was set up, with headquarters at Suva, and the Director of Fiji Medical

Services was appointed Central Medical Authority for the Commission to provide unified services for all British colonies in the region. Following a survey mission of medical experts to the South Pacific in 1943, P. E. Mitchell, Governor of Fiji, wrote to the Secretary of State for the Colonies in London, proposing a strengthened medical and public health system for Fiji, including the idea of a Health Center for the South West Pacific that might have its own medical and nursing services. In early 1944, the proposal was reshaped as a joint Public Health and Medical Service for Fiji and the Western Pacific under a Director-General, with the understanding that the Service might evolve into a regional health authority of some sort. As the Rockefeller Foundation seemed interested in providing funds and had proposed a joint medical service as early as 1922, the British Colonial Office developed the idea of a Joint Pacific Medical Service, with a Joint Board, and New Zealand was approached for support. When New Zealand endorsed the proposal in February 1944, the projected title was Joint Pacific Public Health and Medical Services, with a Pacific Public Health Board as administering authority. In March 1944, terms of reference were drawn up for the Joint Pacific Public Health and Medical Service and South West Pacific Board of Health with Fiji, with the Western Pacific High Commission, New Zealand and its dependencies, including Western Samoa, as future participants. By May the proposal was first for a South Pacific Medical Service, then for Pacific Medical and Health Services. In June 1944, when Australian participation in the scheme was being sought, the proposal was retitled as a South-West Pacific Medical Service, with a South-West Pacific Board of Health. But these titles were rejected.

On April 1, 1945, Fiji, New Zealand, and the Western High Pacific Commission (representing the British Solomon Islands and the Gilbert and Ellice Islands) met at Suva to establish a headquarters for the South Pacific Health Service (SPHS). The position of Director of Medical Services in Fiji was combined with that of Inspector-General of the South Pacific Health Service on September 1, 1946. The entire arrangement was then formalized by the Agreement for the Operation of a South Pacific Health Service on September 7, 1946, in which the organization was primarily "to advise the participating Administrations on all health matters within their territories..." (par. 7a) "in the more effective control of disease and promotion of health within the...Territories" (par. 7i). On January 1, 1947, when Tonga was added to the countries involved in the service, the arrangement became somewhat more than a bilateral New Zealand-United Kingdom colonial effort and thus the South Pacific Health Service developed into one of the earliest regional international organizations in the South Pacific.

SPHS was operated by the South Pacific Board of Health, which originally had six members: the Inspector-General, South Pacific

Health Service; the Fiji Director of Medical Services or, when that post was held by the Inspector-General, a person nominated by the Governor of Fiji; the Director-General of the New Zealand Department of Health or his representative; the Director of the Nursing Division of the New Zealand Department of Health or her representative; a person appointed by the High Commissioner for the Western Pacific; and a representative of the International Health Division of the Rockefeller Foundation (eliminated in 1958). Tonga was allotted a seat in 1947, and Western Samoa in 1958.

The Inspector-General was the chief administrative officer of the SPHS and chaired the Board (Figure 2.1). The Board, with a Headquarters in Suva, met on an annual basis, usually for two-day sessions; all decisions were by majority vote. Up to 1956 the annual meeting of the Board was just before the annual meeting of the Central School of the Medicine Advisory Board. In 1962 the latter changed its name to Fiji School of Medicine Advisory Board, and the two bodies met separately in 1963 and thereafter.

The Inspector-General was subject to the authority of the Governor of Fiji (and the High Commissioner for the Western Pacific up to 1958), and was appointed by the British Secretary of State for the Colonies in consultation with the New Zealand government. The Board employed a modest professional and clerical and office staff. The Inspector-General, a medical practitioner, was responsible for arranging the temporary secondment of medical and health personnel to the territories covered by the health service, as needed to operate the various programs of SPHS. The position of an Assistant Inspector-General, also a medical practitioner, was authorized by the 1958 agreement but was left unfilled for much of the time.

The initial agreement of 1946 was between three governments (Table 2.1): the Colony of Fiji, New Zealand (on behalf of its island territories), and the Western Pacific High Commission (on behalf of British island territories). Later in 1946, Tonga requested to be included, and the existing members agreed to do so as of January 1, 1947. Subsequently, when Western Samoa neared independence, it asked to be added as a new member. Fiji became independent in 1970 and thus was never a member of SPHS as a sovereign state. Australia decided not to participate, though its support was solicited. In 1952 the Western Pacific High Commissioner moved from Fiji to Honiara in the British Solomon Islands (when the position of the Fiji Governor was no longer identical to that of the Western Pacific High Commissioner), but still had jurisdiction over the Gilbert and Ellice Islands Colony (later renamed Kiribati and Tuvalu, respectively). Therefore, Gilbert and Ellice Islands decided to send an observer to the Board in 1967. The New Hebrides (now Vanuatu) sent an Observer to the final meeting of the

Figure 2.1
Organization of the South Pacific Health Service

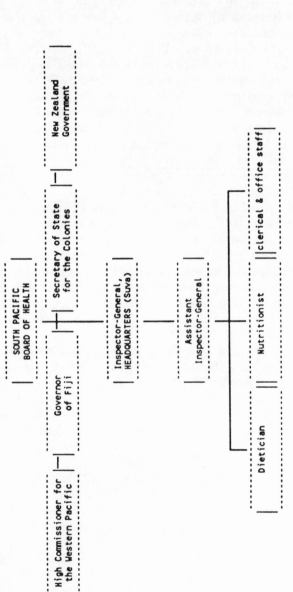

Table 2.1
South Pacific Health Service: Membership and Finances

Year Joined	Member Countries	Contribution (1969)
1946	Fiji	43.8%

	New Zealand (on behalf of
	  Cook Islands,
	  Niue,
	  Tokelau Islands,
	  Western Samoa)
		12.5

	Western Pacific High Commission
	  (that is,
	  British Solomon Islands,
	  Gilbert & Ellice Islands)
		25.0

1947	Tonga	6.3
1957	Western Samoa	12.5
Totals	defunct in 1969	$13,589

Board in 1969. Activities of SPHS, nevertheless, covered other countries and territories. The medical school in Suva received students from Nauru, New Hebrides (Vanuatu), and Papua New Guinea, in addition to those of the member countries. The epidemiological service extended to American Samoa, French Oceania, Netherlands New Guinea, New Caledonia, and Papua New Guinea. Information was also exchanged with Guam, Hawaii, and the Trust Territory of the Pacific Islands.

In 1946 the budget of SPHS was F£2,988 (US$7,524). By 1969 expenditures rose to F$15,627.18 (US$13,589). The contribution formula was evidently based on the relative size of populations served by each member (Table 2.1). External funds were used to defray special projects, as noted below. Medical officers' salaries were usually paid by the receiving island administration; in the case of secondment, the receiving administration often paid transport charges. All nurses were paid by the New Zealand government.

The founding Agreement charged SPHS with several specific responsibilities. One was the need to maintain a pool of medical officers and nurses for assignment to positions in the island countries. In 1949 there were 24 medical officers and about 100 nurses in the pool, all recruited from New Zealand. The procedure was to give contracts to medical and nursing personnel for work in the Colonial Medical Service in Fiji; they were then nominally appointed to SPHS and available for secondment to the various participating territories. Fiji personnel were also seconded under the arrangement. The yearly count of personnel available for assignment was discontinued in 1960, as it was no longer deemed necessary.

What happened to improve the situation was the training of medical and nursing personnel, either at Central Medical School, Nurses Training School in Suva, or at various institutions in New Zealand and the United Kingdom. Nurses continued to be trained in local hospitals and went to Suva only for certain special courses.

A third major project was an epidemiological service; a yearly count of those afflicted by various diseases in the island nations was published by SPHS. Research on specific diseases was monitored by SPHS on a continuing basis.

Other projects included installing water-seal latrines; providing rural water supplies, immunization services, family planning assistance, and clinical services; and preparing health education materials in local languages, a quarantine reporting code, and a program in nutrition and hospital food.

The founding Agreement called upon the Inspector-General to cooperate with "Regional Health Bureaus," a provision that was clarified in 1958 to mean the South Pacific Commission (SPC) and World Health Organization (WHO). The Board discussed WHO programs regularly, and WHO sent an Observer to Board meetings from 1966 to 1969. The WHO Regional Office for the Western Pacific, still headquartered in Manila, originally had a South Pacific Area Office in Sydney. The transfer of the WHO South Pacific Area Office from Sydney to Suva in 1968 meant that WHO programs were to be provided more efficiently to the South Pacific region.

SPC also attended the final two Board meetings. SPHS was concerned about possible duplication with SPC from the latter's inception; no formal method for coordination was ever established, but discussions were frequent, and the SPHS Inspector-General was for a time a member of the SPC Research Council. In 1961 SPC convened the Conference of Directors of Territorial Health Services in order to set priorities for its activities in the health field, and eventually SPC established an epidemiological survey with a scope that extended beyond SPHS countries; the obvious duplication of effort prompted SPHS to devolve responsibility to SPC for the entire region. When the second SPC meeting of health directors was held in 1971, SPHS had already been terminated. The SPC-convened conference is known today as the Regional Conference of Permanent Heads of Health Services.

Meanwhile, the Fiji School of Medicine developed into a regional training center, as SPHS had hoped. Accordingly, member countries of SPHS agreed in 1969 that the organization's functions were being performed ably by other institutions, and thus SPHS could be terminated on a positive note, its work having successfully upgraded public health in the region to the point where outside assistance would henceforth be needed only as a supplement to existing national island public health services. The Pacific Way was an inchoate concept during the life of SPHS, and by the time it took form basic medical needs in the region had been met.

SOUTH PACIFIC AIR TRANSPORT COUNCIL[2]

In 1944 meetings were held with a view to establishing the International Civil Aviation Organization (ICAO) as one of the new Specialized Agencies of the United Nations. Delegates from Commonwealth countries had informal conversations at the Montreal conference regarding ICAO in October 1944. Then discussions on the idea continued in December 1944, when Commonwealth countries met on their own. One result of these efforts was the formation of the Commonwealth Air Transport Council (CATC), which had its inaugural meeting at London in July 1945.

Meanwhile, when World War II ended, the principal means of air travel in the South Pacific was by military aircraft. Civilian facilities were either antiquated or had been damaged. Military facilities established by the U.S. Air Force during the war were converted to civilian use, but no government was responsible for postwar civil aviation. On December 20, 1946, New Zealand was scheduled to resume control over Nadi airport, Fiji; new air services were needed to link Australia with New Zealand as well as Australia and New Zealand with the United States, with Nadi as a refueling stop en route. During the July 1945 meeting establishing CATC, the Committee on Commonwealth Air Routes noted the success of the South African Air Transport Council and suggested that a Regional Council should be set up for the southwest Pacific along the same lines.

At a meeting in Canberra on December 13, 1945, Australia and New Zealand gave further consideration to the idea. Within the framework of CATC, accordingly, the Civil Aviation Conference of February 28 to March 5, 1946, was convened at Wellington, where Ministers of Civil Aviation from Australia, New Zealand, and the United Kingdom drafted the Constitution for the South Pacific Air Transport Council as well as for two subsidiary bodies, the Committee for Air Navigation and Ground Organisation (SP CANGO) and the South Pacific Committee of Meteorologists (SP COMET). (The "SP" prefix referred to the fact that CATV had committees with identical names.) Although SPATC was set up under the aegis of CATC and was a subordinate organ of CATC in principle, in fact it operated quite autonomously. SPATC's Constitution was revised over the years but was best summarized by its first function, namely, "to keep under review and to promote the progress and development of Commonwealth civil air communications in the South Pacific and on the main trunk air routes traversing that area."

The plenary organ (Figure 2.2)—attended by ministers of civil aviation, the Governor of Fiji, and the Western Pacific High Commissioner—was the Council, which held annual meetings of about five days until the 1960s, when meetings at less frequent intervals were preferred. The Permanent Chairman of the Council was Australia's minister of transport, though the Chairman at each meeting was designated by the country in which the meeting was held.

The Council, in turn, established a complex structure of committees relating to technical and policy matters. SP CANGO took over the functions of SP COMET in 1952, then returned in 1955 as the Regional Aviation Services Technical Committee, and SP COMET was revived as the Meteorological Committee in 1962. The inaugural Council set up an ad hoc Policy Committee to review air services. The Policy Committee recommended the formation of two new airlines, British Commonwealth Pacific Airlines and Trans-Empire Airways, but these operated outside the scope of SPATC. To watch over these new carriers, two SPATC committees were formed: the Trans-Pacific Committee, with headquarters at Canberra, to plan and coordinate air services from the South Pacific to North America; and the Trans-Tasman Committee, headquartered at Wellington, to look at the operation of air services between Australia and New Zealand. The latter committee superseded the former Tasman Air Commission on March 31, 1947. In 1948 the two committees, redefined jurisdictionally to operate outside the scope of SPATC, still reported to the Council as a matter of courtesy and convenience, but were superseded by the Finance Committee (SP FINCO), which eventually became the most powerful body of the organization, reporting to the council in the years when it met, and reporting directly to member governments in the other years.

The Council established a Secretariat for SPATC in Melbourne, which was provided by the Air Transport Group of Australia's Department of Transport. A Secretary was in charge.

Although the original proposal was for an organization to include Canada, four members were involved initially (Table 2.2). Two new members and two Associate Members joined in later years. Canada, an Observer in 1946 and 1947, joined until 1965 and then withdrew. When the office of the Western Pacific High Commission moved to Honiara in 1952, Fiji was considered to be a new member, and it undertook the responsibility of representing Tonga from 1952 until 1973. Chile was represented at the Council meeting in 1948; when SPATC did not adopt its proposal for air service from the South Pacific to South America, it failed to attend further meetings. The United States sent observers in later years. Western Samoa was invited to

Figure 2.2
Organization of the South Pacific Air Transport Council

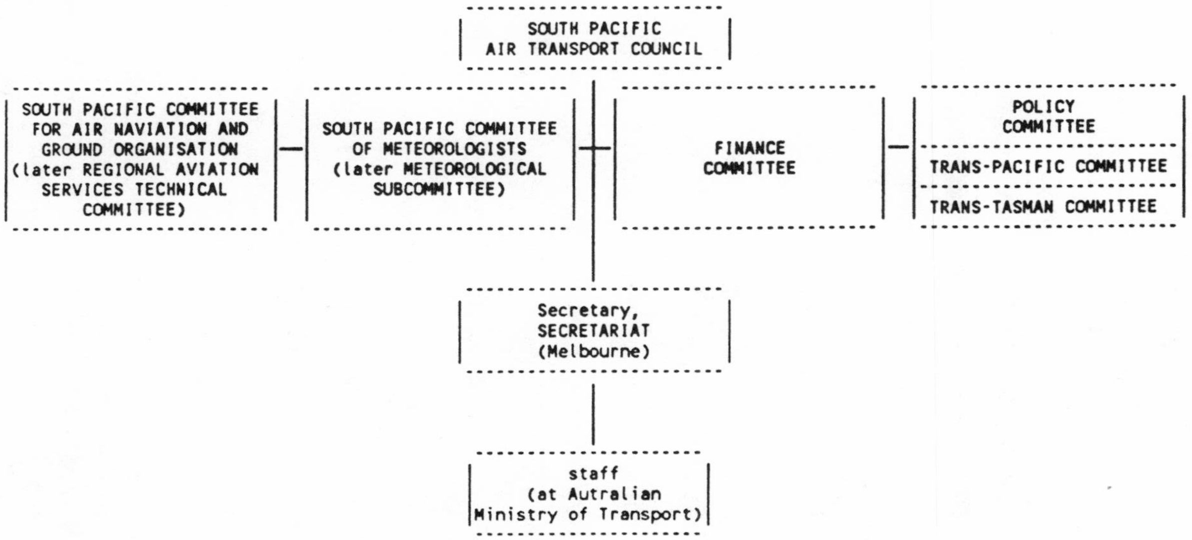

Table 2.2
South Pacific Air Transport Council: Membership and Finances

Year Joined	Member Countries	Contribution (1979)
1946	Australia	33.3%
	Western Pacific High Commission[a]	12.5
	New Zealand	20.0
	United Kingdom	46.7
1948	Canada (withdrew 1965)[b]	
1952	Fiji[c]	
1973	Nauru (Associate Member)	
	Tonga (Associate Member)	
Totals	defunct in 1979	$5,040,000

[a]In addition to representing British Solomon Islands and the Gilbert and Ellice Islands throughout, represented Fiji up to 1952.
[b]Previously represented by an Observer.
[c]Represented Tonga from 1952 to 1972.

become a member but declined. Other observers came from various airline and telegraph companies operating in the region.

Both the Trans-Pacific Committee and Trans-Tasman Committee had a representation separate from SPATC. Only Australia, New Zealand, and the United Kingdom were represented on the two short-lived committees.

Operations of SPATC initially involved reestablishing civilian air services in the Pacific. Funds were placed into two pooled accounts so that the two services (trans-Pacific and trans-Tasman) would have sufficient initial capitalization. In due course, the two air services were sufficiently established so that SPATC was no longer responsible for the capitalization of commercial flights in the region.

Initially, funding for SPATC was on an item-by-item basis, as the start-up facilities were refurbished or put into place. In 1947 the largest item was F£412,428 (US$1,038,570) for the renovation of the Nadi airport. By 1979 the estimated expenditures were about F$6 million (US$5.04 million), defrayed on the basis of a contribution formula in which the United Kingdom paid nearly half of the costs, Australia one-third, New Zealand one-fifth, and the remaining one-eighth came from the budget of the Western Pacific High Commission (Table 2.2). Before SPATC folded, a Fiji debt of A$800,000 (US$672,000) to Australia for capital expenditures at Nadi airport was waived.

The main projects in the early years of SPATC were connected with the establishment of air services by two government-sponsored airlines, British Commonwealth Pacific Airlines and Tasman Empire Airways, which were monitored by SPATC until they were superseded by other carriers. In 1948 SPATC also approved service of Canadian Pacific Airlines to the South Pacific.

Renovation, operation, and maintenance of the airport at Nadi, Fiji, was an integral part of SPATC operations throughout the life of the organization. Initially, the airport was converted from a military landing field under control of the U.S. Air Corps into a major refueling stop on the route from California to Australia and New Zealand. New Zealand was primarily responsible for operating Nadi airport, but various services were transferred to the Fiji government as personnel were trained to assume responsibility in specific functional areas, starting in 1964. The Council agreed in 1973 to transfer full responsibility for Nadi to the Fiji government by July 1, 1975.

Originally, SPATC had responsibility for air traffic to the Gilbert and Ellice Islands (Kiribati and Tuvalu), New Hebrides (Vanuatu), and the Solomon Islands. In 1948 air services to the Solomons were assigned to the Western Pacific High Commission, which was then headquartered in Fiji. Meteorological services for Port Vila, New Hebrides, were transferred from SPATC to joint French-British control in 1955. In due course, meteorological and telecommunication services were provided to other airports in the region, including Kiribati, Nauru, the Solomon Islands (the later headquarters of the Western Pacific High Commission), and Tonga. Australia and New Zealand established programs to train local personnel in Fiji and the Solomon Islands so that the two countries would be able to operate their own civil aviation services after they achieved independence.

In 1961 the Regional Office of ICAO at Bangkok, Thailand, organized the first in a series of annual Informal Meetings of the Directors General of Civil Aviation, Asia and the Pacific (DGCA), a body that serves to review policy and technical matters in the field of civil aviation; SPATC countries have been represented on a regular basis in these meetings. In 1976 the South Pacific Regional Civil Aviation Council (SPRCAC) was launched under the aegis of the South Pacific Forum with the mission of rationalizing civilian air transport for island nations of the South Pacific. Accordingly, SPATC considered that its work had been completed by 1978, when the Council met for the last time. In 1979 SPATC was disbanded.

To some extent, DGCA and SPRCAC continue today the excellent work begun by SPATC some four decades ago. However, only the latter embodies the spirit of the Pacific Way.

CONCLUSION

Although SPHS and SPATC properly considered their organizations to have been successful, there is another side of the story. The proud nations of the South Pacific continued to exert pressure for a speedy transfer of functions from colonial to local personnel while both organizations operated. Assuming sovereign control was an end in itself. The Pacific Way could not fully operate until all vestiges of colonialism were removed. No proposal for a new island-controlled regional organization in the field of public health has been discussed since 1969, and the South Pacific Regional Civil Aviation Council under the Forum has encountered the fundamental problem that each country in the region prefers to operate its own independent airline rather than depend on an air carrier operated even by a South Pacific neighbor. Something may emerge as the Pacific Way harmonizes policies of the region and transforms jealous preferences for sovereign control into pragmatic considerations of the costs and benefits of joint regional action; these issues will be discussed in later chapters.

NOTES

1. Basic information may be found in South Pacific Health Service, *Inspector General's Report* (Suva: South Pacific Health Service, annually, 1947–1969); *Minutes of the Meeting of the South Pacific Health Service* (annually, 1947– 1969).

2. Basic information may be found in South Pacific Air Transport Council, *Report of the Meeting* (Melbourne: South Pacific Air Transport Council, annually, 1946–1978).

3 A PATERNALISTIC ANOMALY FADES AWAY: SOUTH PACIFIC COMMISSION

ORIGINS[1]

Much of the Pacific theater of World War II centered in areas governed by the United Kingdom but under actual Japanese control; the Allied Powers were defended primarily by the armed forces of Australia, New Zealand, and the United States. As U.K. influence in the region was considered likely to decline after the war, Australia and New Zealand began to think of new regional arrangements for the postwar era to fill the void. At the Conference on Wartime and Post-War Cooperation of the United Nations in the Pacific and the Far East, sponsored by the Honolulu-based Institute of Pacific Relations at Quebec in December 1942, Lord Hailey of the British delegation proposed a new organization that could maintain peace in the region while promoting economic development; his suggestion was for a Pacific Zone Council, which might serve as a local office of then-proposed United Nations. The idea particularly appealed to several leaders in Australia and New Zealand, who were impressed with the model of the Caribbean Commission, which had been established in 1942. William Forsyth of the Australian Ministry of Foreign Affairs, who later became Director of the South Pacific Commission, proposed the idea of an economic and social commission for the region, and Herbert Evatt, Australia's foreign minister was attracted by the geopolitical implications of the proposal. Accordingly, the text of the Australia-New Zealand Agreement (the ANZAC pact) of January 1944, included a proposal for a South Seas Commission, and when the Australia-New Zealand Conference met during November 1944, they called for a South Seas Conference to set up a South Seas Commission as a regional equivalent to the Caribbean Commission.

Although the idea was discussed at the May 1944, Commonwealth Prime Ministers' Conference, it was not until after the United Nations was established in June 1945, that plans for the South Seas Conference could be discussed with the other colonial powers of the region, who awaited the finalization of the UN trusteeship system before proceeding to consider regional arrangements. The favorable reception of the proposal for a South Seas Conference at the Commonwealth Prime Ministers' Conference in May 1946, led to the convening of the South Seas Conference at Canberra on January 28, 1947. By February 6, 1947, the six colonial powers in the region (Australia, France, New Zealand, the Netherlands, the United Kingdom, and the United States) had agreed on a framework for the new South Pacific Commission (SPC) and signed the Agreement Establishing the South Pacific Commission, known as the Canberra Agreement.

STRUCTURE

According to the Preamble to the Canberra Agreement, the principal aim of the South Pacific Commission is to "encourage and strengthen international cooperation in promoting the economic and social welfare and advancement of the peoples of the non-self-governing territories in the South Pacific region." As SPC grew, the number of non-self-governing territories fell. Although the Preamble was never amended, it became anomalous in its paternalistic approach to the region. Article IV reiterates the role of the organization in regard to "economic and social development" and the "welfare and advancement" of the peoples of the region and gives specific powers to the organization in regard to undertaking studies, making recommendations to the countries of the region, and providing technical assistance, including coordinating and operating local projects.

Initially, a Session of the South Pacific Commission was the supreme organ of the organization, with a Senior Commissioner and other members of delegations from each country acceding to the Canberra Agreement (Figure 3.1). The South Pacific Conference, the Research Council, and the initial Working Committee were originally set up as special advisory bodies to the Commission.

The structure changed as the locus of power shifted from the colonial powers as the newly independent island nations began to eclipse SPC through the South Pacific Forum after 1971. In order to avoid complete collapse, Australia took the leadership in forging many compromises and reforms in SPC operations. For example, Commission meetings, composed initially of the six colonial powers of the region, were held

Figure 3.1
Organization of the South Pacific Commission

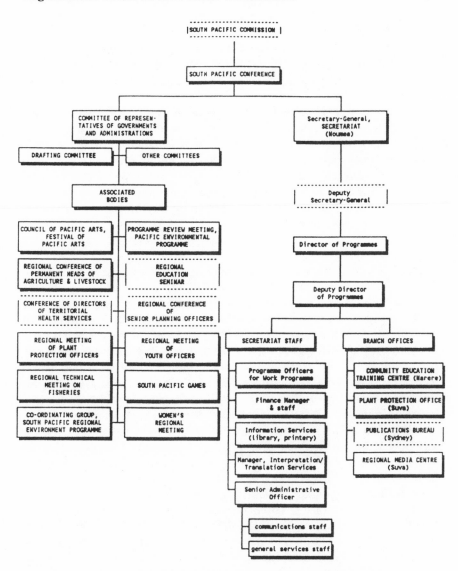

at different times and places from those of the South Pacific Conference, where the colonies were paternalistically allowed to react to the work of the Secretariat; in 1967 the two meetings were scheduled together. By 1973 this paternalism ceased, as the Commission was abolished; the plenary body has been the South Pacific Conference since 1974. The colonial powers then set up the Committee of Representatives of

Participating Governments in 1974 as a screening body for the Conference in matters of a budgetary and constitutional nature, but in 1983 this paternalistic anomaly was superseded by a committee-of-the-whole with the new name Committee of Representatives of Governments and Administrations (CRGA). The island nations of the South Pacific have been in control ever since, though the staff is still primarily from metropolitan countries due to the technical character of the Work Programme.

A Secretariat, headed by a Secretary-General and Deputy Secretary-General, was temporarily located in 1947 at Sydney. Two years later the headquarters moved to Noumea, New Caledonia, except for the Publications Bureau and the Social Development Section, along with the latter's Literature Bureau. In 1956 the Social Development Section moved to Noumea, but the Literature Bureau remained in Sydney. In 1962 the Literature Bureau was absorbed by the Publications Bureau, which in turn was abolished by 1988. The Deputy Secretary-General position was vacated in 1987. There are approximately 100 employees at Noumea today.

Three branch offices currently in Fiji are the Community Education Training Centre, the Plant Protection Office, and the Regional Media Centre. The Community Education Training Centre, established in 1963, operates two mobile training units; the Mobile Home Economics Training Unit, which started in 1947 as a part of Secretariat activities, was integrated with the Centre in 1978. The Centre moved down the road from Suva to Narere in 1987. The Plant Protection Office began as a Section within the Secretariat as early as 1967; when it moved to Suva in 1976, it was upgraded to an Office. The Regional Media Centre was established in 1974 as a consolidation of the Audiovisual Office and the Educational Broadcast Office, which were set up at Suva in 1971. In 1974 the Regional English Teaching Centre was established at Suva, when the language teaching specialist position was reassigned from Sydney to Suva. However, in 1980 the Teaching Centre was reorganized as the English Teaching Materials Unit and was transferred to Noumea. The staff at Suva number about 30, and there are ten persons stationed at various mobile units and research stations in various countries, including a liaison office at Sydney, bringing the total SPC employees to about 140.

Originally, the Secretariat was supposed to handle routine administrative matters, leaving special studies to the paternalistic guidance of the South Pacific Research Council, which had three Programme Directors—for Economic Development, Health, and Social Development. In time the Secretariat began to take on more research-related functions. Accordingly, in 1967 the Research Council was superseded by a Programme Research and Evaluation Council within the Secretariat (consisting of the three Programme Directors and the Secretary-General), but this anomalous body was given little prominence and eventually ceased to function. In 1977 the three Programme Director positions merged into a single Director of Programmes, with a Deputy Director of Programmes assigned primarily to administrative supervision. A Senior Administrative Officer now shoulders the administrative burden, assisted by a Finance Manager, information services staff, and a Manager of Interpretation/Translation Services.

SPC has sole or joint responsibility on behalf of several associated bodies of senior-level officials. The Conference of Directors of Territorial Health Services began in 1961, reconvened in 1971 for annual meetings until 1976, and last met in 1979 and 1981. The Regional Education Seminar was held on an annual basis from 1969 until 1980. The Regional Conference of Permanent Heads of Agriculture and Livestock Production Services began in 1972. SPC is Secretariat for the Council of Pacific Arts, which started in 1977 to coordinate the annual Pacific Festival of Arts. Although SPC organized the South Pacific Games initially, they now operate autonomously. SPC is a member of the Co-ordinating Group for the South Pacific Regional Environment Programme (SPREP), formed in 1979 along with the South Pacific Bureau for Economic Co-operation (SPEC). The Regional Conference of Senior Planning Officers, another joint project with SPEC, began in 1982 but lapsed by 1987. The Pacific Environmental Programme (PEP) began in 1983, with a Programme Review Meeting in a coordinating role. Other bodies include the Regional Meeting of Plant Protection Officers, Regional Technical Meeting on Fisheries, Regional Meeting of Youth Officers, and the Women's Regional Meeting, which comment on SPC's Work Programme in these fields.

MEMBERSHIP AND FINANCES

The Canberra Agreement was signed in 1947 and ratified by six countries in 1948 (Table 3.1). Colonies in the region were designated as Administrations or Territories and were paternalistically considered ineligible for membership. Tonga was the only island nation with its own constitutional autonomy in the South Pacific at the time, never having been formally colonized. The six SPC countries repeatedly urged Tonga to ratify the Agreement, but it refrained from doing so even after its formal status as a British protectorate was terminated in 1970. Tonga considered the structure of SPC—rather than its own refusal—to be the anomaly. In 1962, when West Irian (Netherlands New Guinea) was transferred from Dutch to Indonesian control, the Netherlands ceased to be a member of SPC. When Fiji, Nauru, and Western Samoa became independent and ratified the Agreement, they

Table 3.1
South Pacific Commission: Membership and Finances

Year Joined	Member Countries	Contribution (1984)
1948	Australia	33.36%
	France	13.90
	Netherlands (nonmember 1962)	
	New Zealand	16.19
	United Kingdom	12.21
	United States	16.88
1965	Western Samoa	.25
1969	Nauru	.25
1971	Fiji	.55
1975	Papua New Guinea	.39
1979	Solomon Islands	.25
	Tuvalu	.25
1980	Cook Islands	.25
	Niue	.25
1983	American Samoa	.55
	Federated States of Micronesia	.39
	French Polynesia	.55
	Guam	.55
	Kiribati	.25
	Marshall Islands	.39
	New Caledonia	.55
	Northern Mariana Islands	.39
	Palau	.39
	Pitcairn Islands	exempt
	Tokelau	.25
	Tonga	.25
	Vanuatu	.25
	Wallis and Futuna	.25
Totals	28-1=27 Members	$2,740,653

qualified for membership on the Commission. After the Commission was abolished the newly ratifying members were allowed to join the Committee of Representatives of Participating Governments of the Conference; eight new members joined in this manner between 1975 and 1980. In 1983 the South Pacific Conference adopted a resolution, providing that all Administrations and Governments represented should have equal and full membership, regardless of ratification or independence status. This brought the full membership to 27 countries, including Tonga, whose conditions were finally met.

SPC's scope was originally confined to territories in the South Pacific within a zone that excluded Guam, Tonga, and the Trust Territory of the Pacific Islands. In 1951 the zone was extended to include Guam and the Trust Territories. In 1975 Norfolk Island and Tonga were added to the zone. The former was removed from the zone in 1980; a Norfolk Island representative attended that year as an Adviser to the Australian delegate, arguing that the island's inclusion in the zone was yet another anomaly, as it had no indigenous population.

Initially, voting on the plenary organ, the Commission, was one vote per member. In 1965, when Western Samoa entered, the allocation of votes was calculated on the basis of a formula based on the number of dependencies ruled by each metropole, with only one vote for Western Samoa. The Commission and later the Committee of Representatives of Participating Governments controlled the number of delegates, alternates, and advisers sent by the Territorial Administrations to the South Pacific Conference through an elaborate formula based roughly on population. In 1983 the Conference finally scrapped the paternalistic system of weighted voting, and all countries now have one vote each. The current distinction among members is between Participating Governments and Territorial Governments.

Other countries have attended meetings of the Commission and the Conference over the years as Observers. These include Canada, Chile, Federal Republic of Germany, India, Indonesia, Japan, Peru, the Republic of China, and the Republic of Korea.

Metropolitan countries defray most of the expenses of the organization (Table 3.1). Initially, a complicated contribution schedule was drawn up for the colonial powers. In 1965, when Western Samoa ratified the Canberra Agreement, it was assessed 1 percent, and New Zealand's share was reduced by 1 percent. The practice, therefore, was to reduce metropolitan-power payments by 1 percent as former colonies ratified. When all countries were admitted to equal status in 1983, a new funding scheme was adopted on the basis of per capita incomes.

Budgets defray costs of conferences, project costs, and branch office and secretariat expenses, with voluntary contributions often paid by metropolitan powers above the level of established contribution requirements. In 1948 the budget was for A$76,340 (about US$190,850). In 1984 the projected expenditures were 470,981,300 Pacific francs (approximately US$2,740,653), of which PF27.3 million came from external sources, PF5.5 million were reallocated from the previous year's budget, and PF108,500 were extrabudgetary contributions for special projects by Australia, France, French Polynesia, New Caledonia, New Zealand, and the United States. As the Publications Bureau in Sydney made a small profit, its surplus funds were reallocated to the English Language Teaching Unit.

PROJECTS

When SPC began, the colonial powers saw their responsibility as facilitating development toward eventual independence by the island countries of the South Pacific. The Research Council was set up to study needs and to recommend projects, and initial categories of attention were economic development, health, and social development. In due course the activities expanded to cover more areas, and in 1976 the focus was specified as follows: ad hoc expert consultation, assessment and development of marine resources, cultural exchange, research, rural development, training facilitation, and youth and community development.

There are about ten work programs today. The Food and Materials Programme has a Family-Level Food Crops and Home Economics Project and projects in the field of plant protection, including training courses, workshops, publications, and the South Pacific Commission Regional Plant Protection Service. The Marine Resources Programme has information services, technical meetings, training, and research on deep-sea fisheries development, focusing on billfish and tuna. The Rural Management and Technology Programme includes the South Pacific Regional Environment Programme (SPREP), as well as efforts to improve rural health and sanitation and to develop rural employment and technology. The Community Services Programme includes the Community Education Training Centre, youth and adult education projects, women's programs and activities, and a wide variety of health-related projects. The Socio-Economic Statistical Services Programme has a Statistics Section, Economic Section, and services in population data and data utilization. The Education Services Programme is divided into the English Language Teaching Unit and the Regional Media Centre and related activities. Information Services involve the library, the Sydney-based Publications Bureau, documentation services, computer services, interpretation and translation, and the use of the communication satellite based at the University of Hawaii, known as PEACESAT. Regional Consultations, considered another aspect of SPC activities, include meetings of the South Pacific Conference, CRGA, and regional conferences in the fields of agricultural and livestock production services, development planning, education, energy, environment, and health, as well as consultations with other international organizations to secure funding for programs. The Awards and Grants Programme provides funds for expert services, research, study visits, and travel grants. The Cultural Conservation and Exchange Programme assists the yearly Festival of Pacific Arts, which began in 1977. Although the South Pacific Games began under SPC auspices in 1963, they are now held outside the framework of the organization. Many of the countries of the region consider the programs to be inconsequential in benefits, though professionally executed—a Western solution to a Pacific problem.

IMPLICATIONS

Clearly, the work of the organization is varied, providing direct input to technical aspects of the ministries of all South Pacific island nations. By pooling expertise, SPC provides services to countries of the region that would be unable to afford these programs. However, personnel at the Secretariat continue to come from outside the region, and the organization has been unable to overcome the paternalistic colonial aura that is so contrary to the Pacific Way.

As a consequence, discussions about the possibility of merging SPC with the South Pacific Forum have been occurring over the last several years. In 1979 SPC accepted the invitation of SPEC to hold annual meetings to facilitate better coordination of their respective programs, and a joint body was established to meet on an annual basis in order to improve coordination. It was then understood that SPC focuses on cultural, scientific, and social activities; SPEC restricts itself to economic questions, Forum Fisheries Agency to fisheries management, and the South Pacific Forum to political issues. SPC is the secretariat for the Convention for the Protection of the Natural Resources and Environment of the South Pacific Region of 1986, which was negotiated through the efforts of SPEC. Yet, the "SPC Way" and the Pacific Way still clash. The nuclear weapons policies of France and the United States, for example, are seen as compromising the integrity of SPC. In 1988 the South Pacific Forum set up the South Pacific Organizations Co-ordinating Committee (SPOCC) to place SPC on an equal footing with SPEC, which in turn was retitled South Pacific Forum Secretariat. As SPC would become subsidiary to the Forum through this innovation, the Conference of SPC deferred acceptance of the arrangement until 1989. The future of SPC appears to consist in having its functions gradually transferred to other bodies where South Pacific island nations have a greater measure of control.

NOTE

1. Basic information may be found in South Pacific Commission, *Report of the South Pacific Commission* (Noumea: South Pacific Commission, annually, 1947–1963); South Pacific Commission, *Report of the South Pacific Conference* (Noumea, annually, 1973–). See also Richard A. Herr, "A Child of the Era: Colonial Means and Ends?," *New Guinea, and Australia, the Pacific and South-East Asia* IX (July, 1974): 2–15; T. R. Smith, *South Pacific Commission: An Analysis After Twenty-Five Years* (Wellington: Milburn, 1972).

4 ANZUS, THE "NONNUCLEAR" ALLIANCE: SECURITY TREATY BETWEEN AUSTRALIA, NEW ZEALAND, AND THE UNITED STATES

INTRODUCTION[1]

Imperial Japan's aggression in the 1930s prompted Australian Prime Minister Robert Menzies to propose a Pacific alliance in 1936. Since London was still responsible for negotiating international agreements on behalf of the Dominion of Australia, the proposal was reiterated at the Imperial Conference on May 14, 1937. When Japan attacked China later the same year, the idea of a deterrent pact had obviously come too late, and the Commonwealth countries in Asia and the Pacific prepared for eventual war with Japan. Australia became empowered to conduct its own foreign relations for the first time in 1940, and it insisted that a Pacific War Council be set up, including New Zealand and the United States, to coordinate military policy in the Pacific. The Council was established at Washington D.C., in 1942, when an Allied Intelligence Bureau was also set up—first at Melbourne and then at Brisbane. The Bureau included military personnel of Australia, the Netherlands, the United Kingdom, and the United States.

Still convinced that the Pacific War could have been deterred by a defensive alliance in the 1930s, the idea for a Pacific pact after World War II continued to motivate leaders in Australia. At the Conference on Wartime and Post-War Cooperation of the United Nations in the Pacific and the Far East, held at Quebec during December 1942, Lord Hailey of Britain proposed a Pacific Zone Council as a regional arm of the then-proposed United Nations, but this idea did not go far enough to suit Australia. In April 1943, Herbert Evatt, Australian Minister for External Affairs, proposed a postwar equivalent to the Atlantic

Charter of 1941. On January 21, 1944, the Australia-New Zealand Agreement, often known as the ANZAC pact, was signed as the first step in the direction of a larger regional arrangement. Then in May 1944, Prime Minister Winston Churchill proposed a Pacific regional council along the lines of the Caribbean Commission that had been established in 1942. The United States was so eager to establish the United Nations as the main basis for postwar peacekeeping that it would not entertain the idea of regional arrangements. In 1945 Evatt nevertheless took a prominent role in drafting provisions of the UN Charter dealing with regional arrangements so that nothing in the Charter could preclude a defensive Pacific pact.

During World War II, the United States used several temporary facilities in Australia and elsewhere throughout the South Pacific. After the war, the U.S. Department of Defense hinted that it wanted to continue using some of the bases. When Australia insisted that any such continued use would only make sense within the framework of a regional security arrangement, the U.S. State Department demurred. Heads of signals intelligence (SIGNIT) agencies, meanwhile, opted for a secret agreement for cooperation in the field of military intelligence between Australia, Canada, the United Kingdom, and the United States, known as the UKUSA Agreement of 1947, which formalized cooperative activities that dated from the early part of the twentieth century; New Zealand joined subsequently.

Australia then continued to pursue the idea of a defense partnership through the Commonwealth, including the Commonwealth Prime Ministers' Conference in 1946. Preliminary Commonwealth talks on the Australian proposal were held in 1949, but several events in 1950 gave greater urgency to the idea of a Pacific pact. After the expulsion of the Kuomintang regime of the Republic of China from mainland China, the Sino-Soviet Treaty of Friendship and Mutual Assistance was signed on February 14, 1950. Two months later, John Foster Dulles was appointed Foreign Policy Adviser to the U.S. Secretary of State with responsibility for negotiating a peace treaty with Japan. The next major event came on June 25, 1950, when the Korean peninsula was engulfed in war. Australia and New Zealand were the first countries to join the United States in sending troops to support the UN Command in Korea.

The events of 1950 required a firm response, in the opinion of the United States. One analysis of the day, to which Dulles subscribed in full, was that occupied Japan had created a vacuum of power, with Communist powers eager to fill the void. Accordingly, a peace treaty with Japan was considered a top priority. Australia and New Zealand, meanwhile, let it be known that they would only be interested in signing a Japanese peace treaty if they were part of a more permanent defensive arrangement involving the United States. Dulles was dispatched to Canberra in February 1951, to meet Australian External Affairs Minister Percy Spender and later Frederick Doidge, New Zealand Minister for Foreign Affairs, to discuss proposals for a defensive arrangement among the three countries. An Australian-U.S. mutual defense assistance agreement was signed in the same month, making Australia eligible for U.S. military aid (New Zealand waited until two weeks after the ANZUS treaty to sign a similar agreement in 1952). Thereafter, Dulles prepared a draft Security Treaty Between Australia, New Zealand, and the United States of America, which was signed at San Francisco on September 1, 1951, and came into force on April 29, 1952, exactly one day after the Japanese peace treaty went into effect. The treaty with Australia and New Zealand was part of the Japanese peace settlement, insofar as it sent yet another signal to Moscow and Beijing that Western-oriented countries were determined to stop new aggressive moves in the Pacific.

In addition, the United States signed separate defensive alliances with the Philippines (1951), Japan (1951), the Republic of China (1954), and the Republic of Korea (1953); and the agreement forming the South-East Asia Treaty Organization (SEATO) in 1954. Because certain circles in the U.S. State Department were anxious to avoid the impression that the trilateral security treaty was to deal with the entire Pacific area, the acronym ANZUS emerged and was accepted at the inaugural meeting of the Council in August 1952. However, Washington wanted Canberra to participate in SEATO, and ANZUS was Australia's *quid pro quo* for agreeing to join SEATO.

The preamble to the ANZUS treaty pledges the three countries to pursue the following principles: "to strengthen the fabric of peace in the Pacific Area" by declaring "publicly and formally their sense of unity, so that no potential aggressor could be under the illusion that any of them stand alone" and then "to coordinate their efforts for collective defense for the preservation of peace and security." Claiming that this set of purposes means that ANZUS is a "nonnuclear" treaty, New Zealand Prime Minister David Lange decided in early 1985 that military vessels, previously allowed to rotate freely from port to port among ANZUS countries, would not be allowed to dock at New Zealand ports unless he was satisfied that they contained no nuclear weapons. As the United States continued its policy of neither confirming nor denying nuclear weapons, the *S.S. Buchanan* was denied access to New Zealand ports. As a result, Washington indefinitely suspended all ANZUS activities involving New Zealand, and in 1986 Australia and the United States jointly agreed to suspend the alliance.

Figure 4.1
Organization of ANZUS

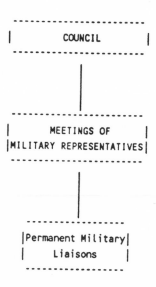

STRUCTURE

The ANZUS Treaty set up a Council (Figure 4.1), consisting of foreign ministers or their deputies, that was to meet to implement the Treaty or at any time, as needed. At the first meeting of the Council, the three countries decided to meet on an annual basis; except for 1960 and 1961, this was the practice until the events of 1985. Deputy members were available in Washington for special meetings so that the three countries would remain in continuing consultation.

Since military considerations are central to the treaty, Meetings of Military Representatives were held within the framework of ANZUS on an annual basis after 1952. While the Council rotated meetings between Canberra, Washington, and Wellington, the Meetings of Military Representatives alternated between Melbourne, Pearl Harbor, and Wellington. The Military Representatives and (after 1955) Staff Planners used their meetings to organize annual military exercises held within the framework of ANZUS.

Although the first meeting of the Council recommended the establishment of a permanent secretariat in Washington, no central office or secretariat was ever created for ANZUS. Secretariat functions for the annual meetings were handled by the Foreign Ministries of the host governments each year. Permanent military liaisons have been the U.S. Commander-in-Chief Pacific (CINCPAC), the Chairman of the

Table 4.1
United States Military Facilities in Australia under ANZUS

Year Started	Year Ended	Location	Name of Function or Project
1955		Alice Springs	Joint Geological and Geophysical Research Station
1957	early 1960s	Woomera	radio tracking stations
1957	early 1960s	Woomera	Baker-Nunn Camera Optical Tracking Station
1958	c.1960	Nauru	weather station construction
1960		Mildura	Project HIBAL
1960		Perth	Project Mercury Radio Tracking Station
1960	late 1960s	Woomera	Deep Space Station 41
1960	late 1970s	Muchea	telemetry and control facility
early 1960s		Daly Waters	seismic installation
1960s		Woomera	Project Hi Star South
1961		Smithfield	TRANET Station (later geodetic & navigation satellite tracking)
1961		Narrogin	Seismic Research Observatory
1960s	late 1970s	Carnarvon	Tracking and Data Acquisition Station
1963		Darwin	Mobile Data Acquisition Station
1963		North West Cape	Naval Communication Station (later Naval Communication Station Harold E. Holt)
1963		Tidbinbilla	Deep Space Station 42 (later Deep Space Station Communication Complex)
1964		Pearce	Partial Nuclear Test Ban Monitoring Station
c.1965		Adelaide	seismic installation
c.1965		Charters Towers	seismic installation
c.1965		Hobart	seismic installation
c.1965		Mundaring	seismic installation
c.1965	1970	Sydney	Riverview Seismic Installation
1965	1975	Amberley	Partial Nuclear Test Ban Monitoring Station
1965	late 1970s	Cooby Creek	Applications Technology Satellite Tracking Station
late 1960s		Honeysuckle Creek	Honeysuckle Creek Tracking Station
1965		Ororal	Space Tracking and Data Acquisition Network Station (later Spaceflight Tracking & Data Network Station)

Table 4.1 continued

1966	Pine Gap	SIGNIT ground station
c.1967	Tennant Creek	Warramunga Seismic Installation
late 1960s	Woomera	Smithsonian Astrophysical Observation Station
1969	Norfolk Island	construction of a radio frequency receiving station
c.1969	Casey	geodetic satellite observation post
c.1969	Cocos Island	geodetic satellite observation post
c.1969	Culgoora	geodetic satellite observation post
c.1969	Darwin	geodetic satellite observation post
c.1969	Heard Island	geodetic satellite observation post
c.1969	Manus Island	geodetic satellite observation post
c.1969	Mawson	geodetic satellite observation post
c.1969	Perth	geodetic satellite observation post
1970	Woomera	launching of sounding rockets
c.1970	Thursday Island	geodetic satellite observation post
1971	Nurrungur	Joint Defense Space Communications Station
1975	Alice Springs	Project Jindalee (over-the-horizon radar)
1975	Christmas Island	Project Flowerless
late 1970s	Tennant Creek	Partial Nuclear Test Ban Monitoring station
late 1970s	Darriman	Omega navigation system
c.1978	Caversham	geodetic satellite observation post
c.1978	Townsville	geodetic satellite observation post
1978	Learmouth	Learmouth Observatory
1978	Geraldton	Temporary Mobile Satellite Laser Tracking Facility
1979	Cockburn Sound	U.S. Navy unit
1980	Yarragadee	Mobile Laser Ranging Facility
1981	Alice Springs	Tracking and Data Relay Ranging Facility
1981	Darwin	U.S. Air Force unit

Chiefs of Staff Committee of Australia, and (until 1985) the Chairman of the Chiefs of Staff Committee of New Zealand.

In 1983, after a review of ANZUS by Australia, the three countries agreed to expand talks to include midlevel and senior officials' meetings. This recommendation was similar to one at the first meeting of the Council in 1952, when it was agreed that foreign ministers' deputies should be available on a continuing basis for meetings in Washington whenever required. Neither effort to provide greater continuity to ANZUS was implemented. Australia and New Zealand continue to cooperate militarily today, as do Australia and the United States, but whether such cooperation occurs within the framework of ANZUS or is based on the ANZAC and Australian-U.S. agreements, respectively, has deliberately been left vague. In public the United States considers New Zealand to have withdrawn from ANZUS in 1985. The door is left open to reactivate the various agreements, as the ANZUS treaty is still in force.

Under ANZUS, the United States has operated several defense-related facilities, either on its own or in joint cooperative arrangements, more with Australia than with New Zealand (Table 4.1). Some 250 sites have been used as portable geodetic-satellite receivers at various times, besides many other stationary installations. Most of the facilities have been operated by agencies of the U.S. government. In 1966 the United Kingdom took over the U.S. role, jointly with Australia as before, at the Partial Nuclear Test Ban Monitoring Station at Pearce Air Force Base. Transit Navigational Satellite (TRANET) Station 112 was jointly operated between 1961 and 1971, when Australia took over full control. In 1974 Australia obtained approval to manage the Alice Springs facility should the United States decide to vacate the facility; in 1978 the station was brought under joint management. Australia became a full partner in the North West Cape facility in 1974, though Australians play lesser roles. Australia took over full control of Project HIBAL (High-Altitude Balloon Atmospheric Sampling), also in 1974. Joint facilities were set up from the start at Pine Gap and Nurrungar.

As regards New Zealand (Table 4.2), a facility at Mt. John was operated under a contract to Canterbury University up to 1977 and then was taken over by the U.S. Air Force. Short-term projects, including an underwater sound propagation project in 1972 (Project Kiwi One), have been conducted in New Zealand from time to time. The future status of these facilities is uncertain.

MEMBERSHIP AND FINANCES

Three countries signed the Treaty (Table 4.3). No provision exists for additional members. Article VIII authorized the Council to main-

Table 4.2
United States Military Facilities in New Zealand under ANZUS

Year Started	Year Ended	Location	Name of Function or Project
1963	1973	Woodbourne	aerospace nuclear test monitoring
1967	1984	Mt. John	Baker-Nunn Camera Optical Tracking Station
c.1980		Christchurch Air-port	landing site for Weedono Communication Unit (U.S. Airport Navy) re Antarctica
1982		Black Birch Range	astronomical observatory
1983		Tangimoana	Defence Communications Unit (SIGNIT sta-tion)
1983		Lower Hutt	OMEGA navigational unit (receiver only)

Table 4.3
Security Treaty between Australia, New Zealand, and the United States:
Membership in ANZUS Organs

Year Joined	Member Countries	Year Inactive
1952	Australia	1987
	New Zealand	1985
	United States	1987
Totals	suspended in 1987	

tain a "consultative relationship" with other countries in the Pacific that might contribute to the security of the region, but no such country has attended ANZUS meetings in an observer role.

Article IV of the ANZUS Treaty refers to the invocation of treaty provisions in the event of an armed attack "on the metropolitan territory of any of the Parties, or on the island territories under its jurisdiction in the Pacific." The United States decided to exclude U.K. territories from the ANZUS Treaty, as Washington did not want the treaty to be applicable to then-ongoing guerrilla warfare in Malaya. In 1962 the "treaty area" was reaffirmed to extend to any island territory in the Pacific under the jurisdiction of the three ANZUS powers. In 1964, when Australian troops were sent to aid Malaysia in the military confrontation with Indonesia, Washington provided assurances that the ANZUS treaty area covered only Papua New Guinea, a colony of Australia at the time. When the ANZUS treaty was signed, there were many such "island territories," but in more recent years only a few countries might appear to be covered by this provision of the ANZUS Treaty, including the successors to the Trust Territory of the Pacific Islands (Federated States of Micronesia, Commonwealth of Northern Mariana Islands, and Palau) as well as the Cook Islands and Niue. In 1965 New Zealand granted self-government to the Cook Islands, and the same status was conferred upon Niue in 1974; under the current arrangement, New Zealand is responsible for the defense of both countries. Although reports of the interest of the Cook Islands in joining ANZUS were circulated in the mid-1970s, it is constitutionally unable to do so, as New Zealand provides for its defense. In 1986 the Cook Islands declared an intention to proclaim the status of "neutrality" in view of New Zealand's exclusion from U.S.-related ANZUS activities; such a declaration of intent has no standing in international law.

Although perhaps outside the framework of ANZUS, the Council in 1984 noted that Australia's development of a Pacific patrol boat to meet maritime surveillance needs in the South Pacific had been accepted by several island nations. The Council also took note that New Zealand had offered military assistance to South Pacific countries whenever so requested.

The first Council meeting agreed that there would be no specific ANZUS budget. Each country defrayed its own expenses in connection with the ANZUS meetings and military exercises. The United States finances military operations at joint defense facilities in accordance with provisions in executive agreements signed for each arrangement. In general, the United States paid for installing new defense facilities, while all three countries kept their soldiers on their own payrolls whenever they were assigned to another ANZUS country. Washington offered discounts to ANZUS partners for the purchase of military weapons; only Australia qualifies for this discount today.

PROJECTS

The main task of the Council was to survey the strategic situation in the region, including developments in Asia and the Pacific. Declarations were issued in the form of annual communiqués.

Military exercises were held on an annual basis under the framework of ANZUS; these were mostly naval operations, though air force participation was also involved. Since 1984 the exercises have involved only the United States and Australia, as Washington in 1986 formally announced that all ANZUS guarantees to New Zealand were cancelled, and Australia has agreed to abide by the spirit of this announcement. In 1985 the Australian government bowed to domestic political objections to cancel participation in a previously planned multiple-warhead missile test, but this action did not provoke a counterreaction by the United States.

Another aspect of ANZUS was "exchange duty," under which military of one country served in the corresponding military service of another, largely for training purposes. Examples of exchange duty operations include research on aerospace disturbances on radio communication, radioactivity in the upper atmosphere, and on weather. The U.S. Geodetic Survey was once assigned to Papua New Guinea under the exchange duty program. Since 1985 no New Zealand armed forces personnel have been on exchange duty in the United States, or vice versa. In 1985, on the other hand, Australia had 124 service personnel on exchange duty in the United States.

Under ANZUS, the United States has provided regular briefings of senior military personnel at the Pentagon on a variety of security-related matters, including aspects of new weapons systems. Intelligence was originally shared, with confidential documents supplied to ANZUS partners. Since 1985 Washington has briefed Canberra but not Wellington; the latter withdrew its Defense Attachés from the United States by 1986. Australia shares its intelligence information with both New Zealand and the United States, but the information supplied to New Zealand is from Australian intelligence sources alone. Australia has pledged not to relay U.S. intelligence to New Zealand.

Joint facilities are primarily for intelligence gathering. The data are seismic, photographic, and signals intelligence (SIGNIT) from satellites. The station at Alice Springs was the first of many seismic installations aimed at gathering data on underground nuclear explosions. Satellite ground stations at Pine Gap, Nurrungar, and Tangimoana provide an early warning capability in the event of nuclear missile launchings or troop movements in battle zones, though the same monitoring capability can be used to detect nuclear weapons tests, naval exercises, and the presence of surface ships inside a country's territorial waters; similar technology can engage in electronic eavesdropping on personal conversations. Both ground stations can relay the information thus gathered to command centers, though the satellites can do so directly as well. Nurrungar differs from Pine Gap and Tangimoana in that it also has command and control functions. The air force base at Darwin is used by observational aircraft to monitor the Indian Ocean.

Support for military operations, mostly in the field of defense communications, is perhaps the most important military function of the joint facilities. The Naval Communication Station at North West Cape communicates with satellites, surface vessels, and submarines. The Omega navigation systems are part of at least eight such stations worldwide, beaming low-frequency radio signals that are of particular use by submarines, though they can be used by aircraft and surface vessels equipped to receive the signals. Project Flowerless was a part of a global American acoustical detection system to track the locations and movements of all submarines in the world through hydrophones at various ocean depths, with data relayed to such possible locations as North West Cape. The TRANET Station was set up to track Transit navigational satellites; today, the installation still uses Doppler tracking to obtain data from geodetic satellites in order to make a precise determination of fixed targets, such as intercontinental ballistic missile silos. Other geodetic satellite observational facilities have used optical and Doppler tracking systems; these enable Cruise missiles, for example, to reach targets with considerable accuracy. The newer facility used by the U.S. Navy at Cockburn Sound is a refueling and resupplying station for ships patrolling the Indian Ocean.

Joint research facilities under ANZUS with marginal defense applications have been operated mainly by the U.S. National Aeronautics and Space Administration (NASA). The earliest facilities at Woomera engaged in radio tracking and optical tracking of satellites in deep space; optical tracking was the objective of the facility at Mt. John. Later efforts at Carnarvon, Cooby Creek, Muchea, and Woomera continued these programs. The research facilities at Honeysuckle Creek and Orroral Valley are closed, with some equipment moved to Tidbinbilla. Only Orroral Valley had potential military implications, as it tracked and logged orbital parameters of satellites and assisted malfunctioning military satellites. Project HIBAL involves the launching of balloons to determine the radioactivity of the upper atmosphere; data gathered in this manner can be used to determine the materials used and level of sophistication of atmospheric nuclear weapons tests in the Southern Hemisphere by France, India, and South Africa. Learmouth Observatory, Black Birch Range Observatory, and Woodbourne Air Force Base projects have measured how sunspots interfere with radio frequencies so that corrections can be made before solar flares impact the earth's ionosphere, thereby ensuring continuously accurate radar and radio transmission.

IMPLICATIONS

As early as 1963, New Zealand Prime Minister Keith Holyoake declared that New Zealand would never store, use, nor acquire nuclear weapons, and in 1969 Wellington was one of the earliest signatories of the Treaty on Non-Proliferation of Nuclear Weapons. An issue raised in 1972 over legal liability for incidents involving U.S. nuclear-powered naval ships (which had docked in 1960 and 1964) was resolved in 1975, when Washington agreed to assume full responsibility. Nevertheless, U.S. naval ships carrying nuclear weapons continued to make regular port calls at Australian and New Zealand harbors. In 1985 New Zealand continued to invite conventional naval ships to dock, but Prime Minister David Lange announced the policy of denying access to ships capable of carrying nuclear weapons unless he received assurances to the contrary, while Washington refused to confirm or deny that such weapons were stored on board U.S. ships. The result is that U.S. naval vessels now bypass New Zealand but continue to dock at Australian ports. When a U.S. naval vessel capable of carrying nuclear weapons docked at Suva, Fiji, on January 6, 1988, some observers believed that the U.S. Navy had indeed found an alternative docking facility at a friendlier port. Tonga has also agreed to receive U.S. ships carrying nuclear weapons.

There is some confusion regarding whether ANZUS exists today. In 1985, as noted above, New Zealand refused to allow the *S.S. Buchanan* the privilege of docking at a New Zealand port; New Zealand believed that ANZUS was nonnuclear and hence that the U.S. government should give assurances that the vessel contained no nuclear weapons. Washington refused to confirm or deny whether the ship was outfitted in this manner. Subsequent cancellation of all ANZUS activities by the United States involving New Zealand did not resolve the issue, and Wellington even gave advance approval in 1987 to all U.S. military aircraft to land at New Zealand airfields, while joint facilities at Tangimoana continue to operate as before. In August 1986, U.S. Secretary of State George Shultz announced that he considered New Zealand formally expelled from ANZUS, though there is no procedure for expulsion from ANZUS, and Australia neither agreed nor disagreed with the statement. The Treaty technically remains in force today, since it has not been repudiated, though the organization has formally ceased activity.

There is no dispute that New Zealand plays an insignificant strategic role in the balance of power among the nuclear superpowers today; the quick U.S. response to Lange's refusal to allow the *S.S. Buchanan* port access provides this evidence. The U.S. government evidently feared that New Zealand's example might spread to other countries, such as Japan, which has a policy similar to that of New Zealand. Rather than acting with more finesse, pressure on Wellington was designed to impress more strategically situated countries that future denials of access to U.S. ships would evoke strong countermeasures from Washington. Nonetheless, the ferocity of the sanctions from the United States against humble New Zealand taught a somewhat different lesson to other countries, namely, that the United States will put its own interests above those of other friendly countries and would prefer even to place the nonnuclear defense of its erstwhile allies in jeopardy if needed to maintain a dominant role in the world.

The first people to learn this lesson were, of course, the New Zealanders, who overwhelmingly preferred to remain in ANZUS, yet also by a substantial majority wanted to keep nuclear weapons out of their territory. An important minority within New Zealand was willing to accept nuclear weapons as a price of maintaining the U.S. nuclear umbrella so that New Zealand could be defended by the United States in case of an attack, as specified in the ANZUS Treaty. United States pressure reduced the size of this political minority considerably; the country as a whole realized that Washington was entirely prepared to abandon a faithful ally on what seemed to be a mere technicality.

Australia learned the lesson next. While prepared to cooperate fully with the U.S. military for the time being, the government commissioned a study on measures for an independent Australian defense (in other words, one that might not need the United States after all). The resulting report by Paul Dibb, subsequently modified and accepted by the government, looks forward to the day when Australia will manufacture its own weapons, provide for its own defense without outside assistance, and thus might be able to charge large sums to the United States for the use of its territory for the various military projects at Nurrungar, Pine Gap, and elsewhere.[2]

Meanwhile, a South Pacific Nuclear Free Zone was declared by treaty in 1986 (following the earlier example of Palau, which placed a nuclear-free clause into its constitution in 1983). The Philippine Constitution of 1987 prohibits weapons. Denmark, Greece, and Spain are reconsidering the advantages and disadvantages of a U.S. military presence. Indeed, Denmark, Japan, and Norway have longstanding policies of denying port access to ships carrying nuclear weapons. The events set in motion by the overreaction of the United States to New Zealand, therefore might eventually lead toward an unraveling of the system of alliances and bases built up by the United States throughout the world since World War II.

Although it is certainly possible for ANZUS to be revived through a change in policy on one side or the other, the style of diplomacy known as the Pacific Way would have preferred congenial consultation and ambiguities in relationships, where all parties are treated with dignity and held in equal respect. Washington's "big stick," thus, has become known in the region as a virtual antithesis to the Pacific Way. One result is the decline of U.S. influence in the South Pacific, while Australia and New Zealand take measures to provide for the security of the island nations of the region. Since the continuation of ANZUS turned on whether it was a nuclear or nonnuclear alliance, in effect history will record that the decision was the latter. The trilateral alliance was torpedoed paradoxically by the very country that preferred ANZUS to be a nuclear alliance.

NOTES

1. Basic information may be found in Australia, Department of Foreign Affairs, *Treaty Series*; Australia, Department of Foreign Affairs, *Current Notes on International Affairs* (now *Australian Foreign Affairs Record*); New Zealand, Ministry of Foreign Affairs, *Treaty Series*. See also Desmond Ball, *A Suitable Piece of Real Estate: American Installations in Australia* (Sydney: Hale & Iremonger, 1980); Joseph G. Starke, *The ANZUS Treaty Alliance* (Melbourne: Melbourne University Press, 1965).

2. Paul Dibb, *Review of Australia's Defence Capabilities: Report to the Minister for Defence* (Canberra: Australian Government Publishing Service, March, 1986). With several modifications, this report was accepted as the official basis for government defense planning in Australia.

5 ORGANIZATIONS CONCERNED WITH THE ADMINISTRATION OF JUSTICE: A PROLIFERATION BASED ON STATUS CONCERNS

INTRODUCTION

Four organizations concerned with the administration of justice exist in the South Pacific. The earliest, the Conference of Commissioners of Police of Australasia and South West Pacific Region (CCPASWPR), started in 1903 as an Australian institution; it became more fully international in the years just after World War II. The Conference of Chiefs of South Pacific Chiefs of Police (CSPCP) began in 1970 to serve more of the needs of island nations. In 1972 the South Pacific Judicial Conference (SPJC) was launched; it is composed of Supreme Court justices. An organization of officials at the level of attorneys general, known as the Pacific Islands Law Officers Meeting (PILOM), was formed in 1981. The four organizations serve differing needs and groups of persons, but all promote a better administration of justice in the region through exchanges of information and views.

CONFERENCE OF COMMISSIONERS OF POLICE OF AUSTRALASIA AND SOUTH WEST PACIFIC REGION[1]

At the beginning of the twentieth century, Australia was a Dominion of the United Kingdom, which was responsible for the system of criminal justice on the Australian continent. In 1903 a conference of police commissioners from the various Australian states convened in Melbourne to explore the possibility of unifying police administration within Australia. In 1921 a second conference was convened with the

Figure 5.1
Organization of the Conference of Commissioners of Police of Australasia and South West Pacific Region

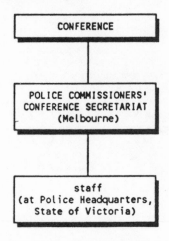

same purpose in mind, and the police commissioners agreed to meet on an annual basis to share experience and information. The group, called the Conference of Commissioners of Police, continued until 1929 but was discontinued with the onset of the Great Depression. In 1937 the Conference resumed, then met again in 1939, 1940, and 1941. Because of World War II, the Conference was again suspended. The next meetings were held annually between 1944 and 1955, and Conferences have been held each year since 1957. The organization has gone through several changes of name since 1903; the present Conference of Commissioners of Police of Australasia and South West Pacific Region has been used consistently since 1977.

The principal aim of the organization is to provide a forum where technical papers on the latest techniques of crime detection and prevention can be presented so that police administrations can be continually improved and modernized. There is no formal charter for the organization, which operates entirely on an informal basis. The annual Conference, the main organ of the organization (Figure 5.1), lasts about five days. Conference sites rotate among member administrations. The central office, the Police Commissioners' Conference Secretariat, is located at Police Headquarters for the State of Victoria in Melbourne.

Initially, the various Australian states (New South Wales, Queensland, South Australia, Tasmania, Victoria, and Western Australia) sent delegations; later the Australian Capital Territory (ACT) and the Northern Territory joined. The Commonwealth also sent a representative from England between 1959 and 1979. Each Australian state and

Table 5.1
Conference of Commissioners of Police of Australasia and South West Pacific Region: Membership

Year Joined	Countries Represented	Year Inactive
1903	Australia	
1939	New Zealand	
1947	Fiji	
1950	Ceylon	1951
1952	Malaya	1953
1958	British Solomon Islands	1959
1959	Papua New Guinea	
Totals	7-3=4 countries	

territory had independent police forces until 1979, when the Australian Federal Police (AFP) was established to deal with federal crimes and to handle police functions in the Australian Capitol Territory. Thereafter, the AFP in Canberra sent a delegation in place of the former ACT and Commonwealth Police Forces. However, the organization was only a national body until New Zealand participated in 1939 (Table 5.1). Fiji, still a colony, sent a delegation in 1948 but did not do so as an independent country until 1971. As this volume defines an international organization to exist only when at least three independent countries are members of a continuing body, the first participation by Ceylon in 1950 enables us to fix a definite date for the internationalizing of the organization. In recent years only Australia, New Zealand, Fiji, and Papua New Guinea have attended on a regular basis. Hongkong sent an Observer in 1983.

Each police administration pays for its own costs of participation. The host administration absorbs costs of renting conference rooms for the meeting. The Victoria Police Headquarters defrays costs of the Secretariat as a part of its administrative budget.

The preparation and presentation of papers on police administration is the main activity of the organization. The high quality of the papers and following discussion is the main attraction of the meeting. At a recent meeting as many as 26 papers were presented, including such topics as fingerprinting, sensor devices, stress in police work, and training programs.

CONFERENCE OF SOUTH PACIFIC CHIEFS OF POLICE[2]

When Fiji became independent in 1970, the Commissioner of the Royal Fiji Police felt that improved police services in the region of newly emerging South Pacific island nations could best be facilitated through a regional effort, based on concepts of the Pacific Way, which were better articulated to the needs of the newly emerging Pacific island nations than the technically sophisticated focus of CCPASWPR. Accordingly, he invited police chiefs from the region to an initial conference at Suva in 1970, and the Conference of South Pacific Chiefs of Police was established.

The main purpose of the organization is to provide an opportunity for exchange of information and experience in police work. In addition, opportunities for exchange of personnel and training are explored and negotiated at the annual meetings. A third objective is to provide an informal network of contacts to facilitate efforts to combat crime when it crosses international waters from one country to another.

There is no formal charter for the organization. In 1979 the Conference at Rarotonga adopted a two-part resolution, setting forth the Responsibilities of the Permanent Conference Secretariat and the Responsibilities of the Host Country. The South Pacific Islands Criminal Intelligence Network (SPICIN) was adopted by a Memorandum of Understanding at the 1987 CSPCP meeting.

The Conference is the main organ of the organization (Figure 5.2); it lasts about five days each year. Each host country provides secretariat facilities for the annual meeting. In 1977 New Zealand was the host country. Although the Cook Islands proposed to hold the next meeting, it was unable to do so until 1979, so New Zealand continued to provide secretariat functions until 1979 and then volunteered to provide a permanent Secretariat for the organization. The 1979 Conference formally accepted New Zealand's offer, and the Secretariat has been in Wellington ever since, at the New Zealand Police Headquarters. The Secretary General of the organization is an Assistant Commissioner of the New Zealand Police, and his duties on behalf of the Conference are added to his responsibilities within his role as a New Zealand police administrator. The annual meetings are now organized by host countries in cooperation with the Secretariat. In 1988 a Control Center for SPICIN was located at Pago Pago; the Executive Director of SPICIN is Deputy Commissioner, Department of Public Safety, American Samoa, who is assisted by seven members of the department.

The host country for the annual Conference has the prerogative of inviting countries to participate. Seven countries attended the inaugural meeting at Fiji in 1970 (Table 5. 2); nine countries, eventually

Figure 5.2
Organization of the Conference of South Pacific Chiefs of Police

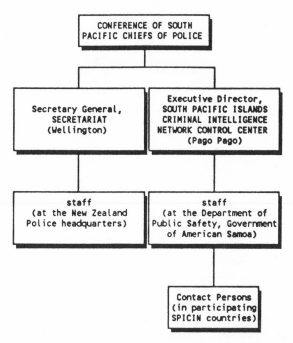

including Australia, joined in later years, bringing the total to 17 countries. Observer status was also accorded to the Trust Territory of the Pacific Islands in 1976 (Northern Mariana Islands in more recent years) and to Hongkong in 1977. An official of the U.S. Drug Enforcement Aqency attended in 1984 in the capacity of Observer, though the United States was not itself recognized as having been represented in the capacity of Observer. Officials from India and the United Kingdom have also attended as Observers in their personal capacity. Fiji, French Polynesia, and New Caledonia participate in CSPCP but not in SPICIN.

Each country defrays the cost of participation by its chiefs of police in the annual Conference. New Zealand absorbs costs of the Secretariat in its national administrative budget. The UN Drug Enforcement Division and the U.S. Drug Enforcement Administration have provided funds for a South Pacific Narcotics Training Program. The UN allotment for training in 1984 was $12,000. Training course tuition is usually paid by the country dispatching students.

The earliest project is the conference itself, where papers are presented and informal discussion on common problems enriches the knowledge of participants. The following topics have been discussed on a regular basis at the various meetings: drugs and alcohol, general

Table 5.2
Conference of South Pacific Chiefs of Police: Membership

Year Joined	Countries Represented
1970	Fiji[a] Kiribati (joined as Gilbert Islands) Nauru Solomon Islands (joined as British Solomon Islands) Tonga Tuvalu (joined as Ellice Islands) Vanuatu (joined as New Hebrides)
1971	Cook Islands New Zealand
1972	Papua New Guinea Western Samoa
1975	Niue
1979	American Samoa Australia[b] French Polynesia[a] New Caledonia[a]
1987	Northern Mariana Islands[c]
Totals	17 countries

[a]Do not participate in the South Pacific Islands Criminal Intelligence Network.
[b]Observer from 1972.
[c]Observer from 1976.

policy, internal police affairs, Pacific problems, police techniques, regional cooperation, and training. Higher-level officials discuss problems of mutual interest, while lower-level personnel attend sessions primarily to receive technical training. Australia, Fiji, and New Zealand have set up programs of college courses for police officers from the region. Personnel exchanges have been negotiated on a bilateral basis to provide training for island nation police officers in the police administrations of Australia and New Zealand.

The South Pacific Narcotics Training Programme, implemented jointly by Fiji and New Zealand, has involved a roving seminar on drug enforcement as well as the preparation of a handbook on the subject for the UN Drug Enforcement Division. With the continued influx of cocaine into the region, SPICIN has established three standardized forms—for the identification of aircraft, suspects, and vessels.

The forms are exchanged with participating countries to aid in law enforcement along with a monthly bulletin.

SOUTH PACIFIC JUDICIAL CONFERENCE[3]

The judicial system in the South Pacific is one of the best integrated among the regions of the world. In times past, judges from Vanuatu (previously New Hebrides) and Western Samoa have presided in Fiji courts, and Fiji judges in turn have been sent to Tonga from time to time. Since 1948, when the Western Pacific High Commission unified rule in one part of the Pacific, appeals from Kiribati, the Solomon Islands, and Tuvalu (as these countries are now called) proceeded first to the Fiji Court of Appeals and then to the Privy Council in London. Meanwhile, Nauru appeals go to London via Australia, and the Cook Islands and Niue route appeals to New Zealand before going on to London. Tokelau goes first to Niue, then New Zealand, then London.

In 1970 the chief justices of American and Western Samoa proposed a Samoan Judicial Conference involving the judicial hierarchy of the two Samoas. As negotiations proceeded, the South Pacific Forum was launched, and the suggestion was made to include attorneys general and justices from New Zealand and the United States as well. Yet another idea was to focus entirely on South Pacific countries. The South Pacific Conference on Law and Law Enforcement resulted, with invitations to the chief justices and attorneys general of some 20 countries for a five-day meeting in January, 1972, which opened in Apia on the 10th and transferred to Pago Pago on the 11th. Meetings of the same group, under the title South Pacific Judicial Conference, have been held ever since, approximately biennially.

The main purpose of the organization is to provide a forum for exchanging ideas. There is no formal statement of objectives, as the meetings operate informally.

The Conference lasts from three to five days. The host country is responsible for secretariat functions. There are no committees or other subdivisions. As some attorneys general are political appointees and others are judicial experts with the same expertise as judges, the 1972 meeting decided to restrict participation to chief justices or their representatives.

The inaugural Conference had 17 countries represented (Table 5.3). Seven countries joined later, though some countries have been unable to attend all subsequent meetings. Although Japan, Malaysia, and the Republic of China have been invited, they have not participated.

Justices finance their own trips and per diem expenses. The host country absorbs local costs of organizing the meeting.

The main focus of the Conference is on the presentation of a series

Table 5.3
South Pacific Judicial Conference: Membership

Year Joined	Countries Represented	Year Inactive
1972	American Samoa	1987
	Australia	
	Cook Islands[a]	
	Fiji	
	French Polynesia	
	Guam	1977
	Hawaii	
	Nauru[b]	
	New Caledonia	
	New Zealand	
	Northern Mariana Islands (joined as Trust Territory of the Pacific Islands)	
	Papua New Guinea	1987
	Tonga	
	United States[c]	
	Vanuatu (joined as New Hebrides)[d]	1982
	Western Samoa	
1979	Kiribati (joined as Gilbert Islands	1987
1982	Federated States of Micronesia	1987
	Norfolk Island	1984
1987	Hongkong	
	Marshall Islands	
	Palau	
	Solomon Islands	
Totals	23-7=16 countries	

[a]Representing Niue since 1977.
[b]Representing Tuvalu in 1987.
[c]Pacific Coast states.
[d]Represented Solomon Islands in 1977.

of papers on legal topics, followed by a discussion led by another justice, who presents a detailed commentary on the preceding paper. The following topics have been discussed in recent years: extradition, immigration, cultural and ethnic aspects in the judicial process, seabed pollution and control, treatment of juvenile offenders, narcotics control, psychiatric evaluation, care of criminal offenders, reciprocal enforcement of judgments throughout the South Pacific, land and titles, air law, law enforcement, law reporting, training of court staff and legal education, a proposed central law library, practice and procedure of Pacific courts, the value of the jury system, common law rules in criminal investigation, fair and speedy trials, private international law, fundamental guarantees in written constitutions, and—a recurrent topic—a proposal for a regional court of appeals. In 1987 the topic was crime control, featuring presentations by a criminologist, a Deputy Committee Chair of a ministerial inquiry into violence, a Deputy Secretary of Justice, a police commissioner, a prison administrator, and a psychiatrist.

The first meeting had both justices and attorneys general in attendance. Due to the shortage of well-trained legal scholars in the region, the justices consisted primarily of expatriates. The attorneys general, on the other hand, tended to be political appointees with considerably less legal experience. The justices felt that their needs for discussion on problems in legal scholarship were at a different level from the practical concerns of law enforcement administrators at the inaugural meeting. The Pacific Way, meanwhile, best described the modus operandi of the attorneys general. As this was not a feasible conjunction of two types of officials, a separate Pacific Islands Law Officers Meeting (PILOM) arose in due course.

PACIFIC ISLANDS LAW OFFICERS MEETING[4]

Since its formation in 1965, the Commonwealth Secretariat has coordinated several ministerial conferences among its member countries. One such conference, the Commonwealth Law Ministers Meeting, is attended by law ministers and attorneys general of Commonwealth countries. As a frequent participant, the Attorney General of Vanuatu felt that a special body was needed to provide services on a regional scale to ministries of justice; he then invited some of the attorneys general of adjacent countries to a meeting at Port Vila in late 1981 to discuss the idea of a regular conference for law officers in the region. Participants at the 1981 meeting, in turn, agreed to form the Pacific Island Law Officers Meeting among both appointed and elected attorneys general in the region and have continued to convene on an annual basis ever since.

The major aim of PILOM meetings is to discuss ways of improving the administration of justice in the countries of the region through the establishment of a regular forum for an exchange of views, through consultation on matters affecting the responsibilities of law officers in their jurisdiction, and through the identification of projects for legal cooperation in the region.

There is no charter. Meetings are held entirely on an informal basis. The host country provides secretariat facilities for the meeting. An agenda is formulated on the basis of papers proposed for the meeting, with the host country coordinating the agenda. Meetings last about three to five days each year.

Any Pacific island country is welcome to apply for membership. Six countries attended the initial conference in 1981 (Table 5.4). Subse-

Table 5.4
Pacific Island Law Officers Meeting: Membership

Year Joined	Countries Represented
1981	Cook Islands
	Fiji
	Kiribati
	Tonga
	Vanuatu
	Western Samoa
1982	Australia[a]
	Nauru
	Papua New Guinea
1983	Tuvalu
1984	Papua New Guinea
1986	New Zealand
	Solomon Islands
1987	Niue
Totals	14 countries

[a]Norfolk Island sent a representative in 1986.

quently, participation has increased to 14 countries. In 1982 representatives from Pacific island countries caucused together in order to consider whether Australia should be considered as an Associate Member; the decision was to treat it as a full member. Tokelau has been invited to PILOM since the 1982 meeting but has yet to attend. American Samoa and Bermuda attended as Observers in 1986. Two organizations are accorded permanent Observer status: the Commonwealth Secretariat and the South Pacific Forum Secretariat.

Each country defrays the cost of participation by its officials at each meeting. Host countries handle conference expenses. The Commonwealth Foundation has assisted in defraying travel expenses for law officers from some of the poorer island countries.

Papers are presented and discussed at the annual meetings. Topics have included conflict between custom and imported law, criminal law and procedure, economic crime and fraud, governmental legal advice, inquisitorial and adversary procedures, legal publications, legal training, legislative drafting, negotiation and execution of international contracts and agreements, patent law, regional legal centers, and treatment of offenders. Reports from island countries are also featured.

The idea of a Pacific law center, discussed at PILOM's meetings, came to fruition in April 1985, when the University of the South Pacific (USP) set up a Pacific Law Unit at Port Vila to provide regular training in law drafting. The USP Pro Vice-Chancellor resigned his position to take charge of the Unit, which receives some funds from the Commonwealth Secretariat.

CONCLUSION

It may seem extraordinary that the South Pacific has four regional organizations concerned with the administration of justice, while Asia, for example, has only one or two such bodies.[5] Status concerns explain the proliferation. Police chiefs supervise police work, attorneys general present evidence gathered by police in court, and judges issue decisions on the cases, so there are three hierarchical levels involved in criminal justice. Judicial independence requires that judges avoid fraternizing with police chiefs, and attorneys general serve in an intermediary role. Yet the fact that there is a similarity in topics discussed as well as the existence of two organizations for chiefs of police—CCPASWPR and CSPCP—suggests additional underlying cultural or economic bases for separate organizations. CSPCP was formed to provide training for police, something unavailable from CCPASWPR; the latter can afford expensive methods of crime detection, while the former cannot. SPJC discusses sophisticated legal theories, while PILOM focuses on formulating cases for trial in a region with a shortage of law clerks. CCPASWPR is "very Australian," while the Pacific Way pervades CSPCP. Foreigners attending SPJC are more comfortable in business suits in air conditioned rooms, while PILOM officials are prepared to roll up their sleeves in a manner consistent with the Pacific Way. Attendance profiles of the four organizations demonstrate that CSPCP and PILOM are serving broad needs within the region, while CCPASWPR and SPJC appeal to the needs of more affluent countries. In 1988 the South Pacific Forum endorsed the Regional Panel of Appellate Judges, thus responding to the shortage of judges in the region as well as the desire to rationalize the appellate system. In due course, as the region confronts more insidious criminal activity and trains more personnel to serve as judges in courts at all levels, the organizations may tend to merge. However, that day will not come until the next century.

NOTES

1. Basic information may be found in Australia, Victoria, Commissioner of Police, *Proceedings of the Conference of Commissioners of Police of Australasia*

and the South West Pacific Region (Melbourne: Commissioner of Police, Victoria, Australia, 1903, 1921–1929, 1937, 1939–1941, annually from 1944).

2. Basic information may be found in Conference of the South Pacific Chiefs of Police, *Minutes of the Conference of South Pacific Chiefs of Police* (annually, 1970–).

3. Basic information may be found in South Pacific Judicial Conference, *Papers* (1972, 1975, 1977, 1979, 1982, 1984, 1987, 1989).

4. Basic information may be found in Pacific Island Law Officers Meeting, *Report of the Meeting of Pacific Island Law Officers* (annually, 1981–).

5. The Asian Judicial Conference (now defunct) and the Meeting of the Chiefs of Police of the ASEAN Countries.

6   *A GOOD DEGREE OF EDUCATION*

INTRODUCTION

As island nations in the South Pacific continue to seek increased control over their own destinies, education is a crucial facet of national planning. The University of the South Pacific (USP) is a unique institution in that there is multinational control of its curriculum and financing so that it can more effectively serve the needs of the region. Since many island countries were colonies of Australia, New Zealand, and the United Kingdom, the primary and secondary educational systems follow the British model of rigorous examinations to determine advancement for each student. The South Pacific Board for Educational Assessment (SPBEA), accordingly, was established to provide technical assistance in the field of educational testing. These two organizations are of concern in this chapter.

UNIVERSITY OF THE SOUTH PACIFIC[1]

When nations of the South Pacific were moving toward independence within the framework of the British Commonwealth, the lack of local facilities for university education was considered a problem to remedy, and the governments of Australia, New Zealand, and the United Kingdom felt that they had a particular responsibility in this regard. Paramedical instruction was available as early as 1886 at Suva Hospital, which was the location of the Suva Nursing School and the Suva Medical School (the latter was renamed the Central Medical School and, by 1961 the Fiji School of Medicine). However, this institution—combined with the Derrick Technical College, Fiji School of Agriculture, and Pacific Theological College—could by no means serve the needs of Fiji after its independence. Meanwhile, Australia founded the University of Papua New Guinea (UPNG) in 1965, and Western Samoa began the South Pacific Regional College of Tropical Agriculture in 1966. Yet the smaller island nations had no institutions of higher learning.

Following consultations between metropolitan and island governments in the region, the U.K. Ministry of Overseas Development in 1965 dispatched the Higher Education Mission to the South Pacific, chaired by Sir Charles Morris with representation from Australia and New Zealand, to assess educational needs in the region. The result was a document issued in May 1966, known as the Morris Report, which urged the establishment of a single University of the South Pacific to be located at the site of the former Royal New Zealand Air Force Flying Base at Laucala Bay, Suva, Fiji, along the lines of the University of the West Indies. The report urged that the new university absorb Derrick Technical Institute, Fiji School of Agriculture, Fiji School of Medicine, and Pacific Theological College. Sir Norman Alexander of the Inter-University Council in London was then appointed Academic Planner to determine the scope and nature of the new university; the subsequent Alexander report of 1967 set down the framework for USP, which excluded existing institutions from its scope. USP was to coexist with the Fiji Institute of Agriculture, Fiji Institute of Technology (formerly Derrick Technical Institute), Fiji School of Medicine, and Pacific Theological College.

An Interim Council for the new University of the South Pacific was first established through a statute passed by the Fiji legislature in 1967, and Sir Norman was named Acting Vice-Chancellor-Designate. A Programme Planning Seminar, held in May 1968, laid down the basic organization of academic activity for the university. After some of the former military base structures were refurbished and students were recruited, USP opened its doors in February 1968. The initial planning period was consummated by the granting of a Royal Charter, formally establishing the University of the South Pacific on February 10, 1970, the same year when Fiji became an independent country.

The preamble of the Charter states that the university exists for "the maintenance, advancement and dissemination of knowledge by teaching, consultancy and research...at appropriate levels...responsive to the well-being and needs of the communities of the South Pacific." The Second Schedule of the Charter, titled Statutes of the University, establishes the basic framework of governance.

The Statutes designate the Chancellor for a term of three years as the titular head of the university who confers degrees (Figure 6.1). The

Figure 6.1
Organization of Governance of the University of the South Pacific

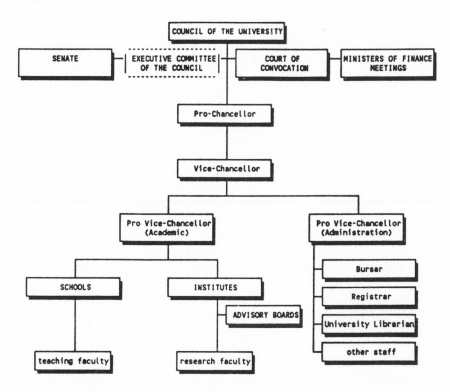

first Chancellor was the King of Tonga. The Pro-Chancellor, who also holds a three-year term, chairs the Council of the University: the Pro-Chancellor tends to be a minister in one of the member countries but today is the Director of the South Pacific Forum Secretariat. The Vice-Chancellor is the chief academic and administrative officer of USP. There are two Deputy Vice-Chancellors, one for academic matters, the other for administration; the former administers the various institutes and schools of USP, while the latter supervises the Bursar, Registrar, University Librarian, and various other support staff. The Office of the Chancellor is the Secretariat of the Council.

The Council of the University has four types of members. The Pro-Chancellor, Vice-Chancellor, Deputy Vice-Chancellor, and Pro Vice-Chancellor are Ex-Officio Members. Appointed Members consist of representatives from each of the founding and other member countries; from the governments of Australia and New Zealand, along with a representative from the American Council of Education; from the Privy Council of the United Kingdom (replacing in 1986 the Inter-University

Council for Higher Education Overseas); and from both the South Pacific Commission (SPC) and the South Pacific Forum Secretariat (as determined by the Council in consultation with the Senate), plus four to six members of the Senate (determined by the Senate in consultation with the Council). Eight persons are Elected Members: three are elected by the Court of Convocation (with at least one from a country in the region other than Fiji), two are elected by the academic staff other than professors, two students are elected by the Students Association of the main campus in Fiji, and one student is elected at USP's Alafua Campus in Western Samoa. However, these Council members have little power. Co-opted Members are selected by the Council to bring persons with experience in agriculture, commerce, industries, the professions, religious institutions, and in such fields as women's affairs. The terms of office vary for each category. Ex-Officio Members are on the Council as long as they hold their offices. Nonprofessional academic staff and students serve a two-year term. All others have three-year terms. The Pro-Chancellor chairs the Council, which selects its own Vice-Chairman from its members, provided that the person selected is neither a member of the academic staff nor a salaried officer of the university.

The Council, the executive governing body of USP, appoints the Chancellor, Vice-Chancellor, and Pro-Chancellor after consultation with the Senate. The Pro-Chancellor presides at meetings of the Council, which selects a Vice-Chairman from its members to serve as an alternate presiding officer. Originally, the Council met once each year, but since the early 1980s it has had two sessions per year; it can also meet in special sessions. Between meetings, the Council may delegate tasks to the Executive Committee of the Council, but this body has not met since the Council decided to have biannual meetings. The Council also maintains standing committees to handle such matters as buildings, finances, resources, and staff policies.

The Senate, academic authority of USP, has increased in power over the years. Its members come from three categories. Ex-Officio Members are the Vice-Chancellor, Deputy Vice-Chancellor, Pro-Vice-Chancellor, heads of Schools, Director of Extension Services, Professors, and the Librarian. Appointed Members are heads and acting heads of academic disciplines, persons from cooperating institutions appointed by the Council, and up to two more persons appointed by the Council. Elected Members come from the academic staff. The Senate has established committees to handle various academic programs. There are three joint committees of the Council and the Senate, which are responsible for appointments, honorary degrees, and staff policy.

The Court of Convocation is composed primarily of USP certificate, diploma, and degree holders, though it also includes all administrators, professional staff, and students enrolled for graduate degrees at USP.

In the early years, when there were few USP alumni, the Registrar added members with diplomas or degrees from other universities residing in USP member countries, but this practice has ceased in recent years. The Court functions to advise the Council, and it selects three members of the Council, but the extent of actual influence is quite limited.

Although the university is run autonomously, it is subject to financial review by triennial Ministers of Finance Meetings to determine the limits of financial commitments from member governments. The Regional Research Advisory Board, composed of heads of agriculture ministries and departments in the region, plays a similar role regarding the Institute of Research, Extension and Training at USP's Alafua Campus in Western Samoa. Institutes at the Laucala Bay Campus have their own advisory boards.

The main campus of USP is at Laucala Bay (Figure 6.2). As of January 1, 1977, the Western Samoa government leased the buildings, equipment, and the land of the South Pacific Regional College of Tropical Agriculture to USP to serve as the second campus site. The college was redesignated as the USP School of Agriculture, and the Institute for Research, Extension and Training in Agriculture was located at the same site. In March 1981, finance ministers agreed to combine the two campus budgets into one, effective January 1, 1982. USP also operates Extension Centres in all Regional Member countries but Tokelau. Four of the research units are located outside Fiji.

The founding Charter calls attention to the interest of 11 Regional Members in the establishment of the university and also allocates seats on the Council to three external donor countries: Australia, New Zealand, and the United Kingdom (Table 6.1). Each country, except for Fiji, has one seat on the Council; Fiji has three in view of its larger share of the budget. Papua New Guinea is not a member, as the University of Papua New Guinea exists to serve the needs of its somewhat larger population, but its Vice-Chancellor has been appointed to USP's Council in recent years. Other seats on the Council can be made available to any major donor organization recognized by USP bodies. Students from Ethiopia, Hongkong, the Maldives, New Caledonia, and Zimbabwe attend, mostly on Commonwealth scholarships.

The United Kingdom agreed to provide up to £1.25 million (about US$3 million) of capital and recurrent costs for the first five years of USP. By 1987 the budget was estimated to be about F$12.5 million (US$11.6 million before the midyear devaluation). As costs were expected to be shared widely within the region, finance ministers of the member countries met in 1971 to determine a formula for cost-sharing. The formula approved in 1971 specified that one-fourth of the cost would be from student fees, one fourth from the Fiji government, and the remainder distributed among Regional Members in proportion to

Figure 6.2
**Organization of Instruction and Research at the University of the South
Pacific**

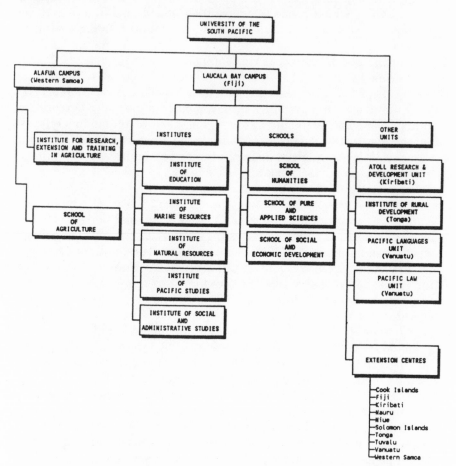

the percentage of students attending USP. The Fiji percentage was
higher than that of other Regional Members because the USP campus
is located on its soil. When the Alafua Campus was added to USP's
structure, this rationale had to be reviewed. In 1981 the finance ministers increased the student portion to 30 percent, apportioned another
30 percent to countries on the basis of their respective percentages of
students (the General Grant), 30 percent to governments in proportion
to the amount paid in salaries to their percentages of the staff (the
Special Grant), and the remaining 10 percent was to be derived from
external sources. Fiji, thus, now defrays 60 percent of the recurrent
expenditures (Table 6.1), though extraordinary contributions have
been made over the years. Australia and New Zealand have provided

Table 6.1
University of the South Pacific: Membership and Finances[a]

Year Joined	Member Countries	Recurrent Expenditures (1987)
1970	Australia	1.47%
	Cook Islands	59.80
	Fiji	2.65
	Kiribati (joined as Gilbert Islands)	0.21
	Nauru	
	New Zealand	0.47
	Niue	4.10
	Solomon Islands (joined as British Solomon Islands)	
	Tokelau	0.49
	Tonga	6.92
	Tuvalu (joined as Ellice Islands)	0.71
	United Kingdom[b]	
	Vanuatu (joined as New Hebrides)	3.21
	Western Samoa	6.32
Totals	14 Members	$11,577,819

[a]Excludes student fees (30 percent) and external grants (10 percent).
[b]Represented by the Inter-University Council for Higher Education Overseas.

funds to support expatriate staff, and institute projects have been financed by Australia, Canada, France, Japan, New Zealand, the United Kingdom, the United States, West Germany, and the Commonwealth Fund for Technical Co-operation (CFTC), European Economic Community (EEC), and the UN Development Program (UNDP).

The primary aim of the university is to educate students. Initially, coursework was limited to the equivalent of junior college level, but in due course each discipline recruited staff to operate a full-fledged academic program. In 1987 some 1,982 students attended USP on a full-time basis, though part-time students numbered 7,455. Bachelor and Master of Arts degrees are available in most fields; certificates and diplomas are offered in some fields as well. In 1987 one person received the Ph.D. degree, seven were awarded master's degrees, 324 received bachelor's degrees, 106 received diplomas, 1 postgraduate certificate, and 134 undergraduate certificates, for a total of 617 degrees in all.

There are seven institutes and three independent research units (Figure 6.2). The Atoll Research and Development Unit studies problems unique to atoll ecosystems. The Institute for Research, Extension and Training in Agriculture engages in agricultural extension, providing training for extension workers and an information network. The Institute of Education services teachers and education ministries. The Institute of Marine Resorces is responsible for research on marine life and undersea minerals. The Institute of Natural Resources promotes the use of local energy, minerals, soils, timber, and water. The Institute of Pacific Studies aims to expand knowledge of regional cultures and societies. The Institute of Rural Development focuses on the need to improve the quality of life of inhabitants of rural areas in the South Pacific through integrated programs of rural development. The Institute of Social and Administrative Studies assists administrators in the region through consultancy and courses. The Pacific Languages Unit specializes in linguistics. The Pacific Law Unit trains paralegal personnel.

The Fiji School of Medicine is operated by the Fiji Ministry of Health. Efforts to formalize a connection between the two institutions by 1986 resulted in an arrangement whereby USP monitors the academic program (appoints the staff, approves the curriculum, and reviews the program) in exchange for serving as the degree-granting institute for Fiji School of Medicine graduates; with the departure of many key staff after the 1987 coup in Fiji, USP may withdraw from this agreement. The University of Papua New Guinea's School of Medicine has offered to accept students whose education is in jeopardy as a result. A less fragile arrangement exists with the Fiji College of Agriculture (whose graduates can then enter the School of Agriculture for a higher degree at the Alafua Campus), the Fiji Institute of Technology, and the Western Samoa Teacher's College. Teaching degrees can also be obtained at the Laucala Bay Campus.

USP has had its share of difficulties since it began two decades ago. Indigenous students often find the excitement of a university education induces them to leave their homelands for better opportunities in more affluent countries. Initially, the staff of USP consisted of many expatriates, who were placed in the position of designing curricula appropriate to a region in which they were only visitors. Rivalry between USP and UPNG is yet another source of tension; only the latter, for example, has a School of Law. The view that Fiji derives disproportionate benefits from USP is reflected in the new funding formula. The use of visa controls on entry to USP positions by the Fiji government is viewed as compromising the regional character of the institution. The Solomon Islands, Tonga, and Western Samoa have indicated an intention to start their own colleges in due course. If other countries open new colleges, the need for USP will decline. USP arose because most countries could not afford a college in the early 1970s; increased prosperity entitles a country to act more autonomously. In 1988 USP was given a seat on the Forum's South Pacific Organizations Co-ordinating Committee (SPOCC), thereby making USP subsidiary to the Forum. The Pacific Way has generally served to smooth over the differences, though no academic institution can claim vitality unless unresolved tensions remain a part of the picture.

SOUTH PACIFIC BOARD FOR EDUCATIONAL ASSESSMENT[2]

One of the difficulties faced by the new island countries of the Pacific has been to evaluate the potential of students for study beyond elementary grades. Teachers are not always in an objective position to make definitive evaluations, as the students often are members of their own extended families. Meanwhile, standard written examinations used in developed countries to determine which students are to receive an advanced education are often inappropriate for the milieu of children and young adults in the region. Since New Zealand was scheduled to grant independence to most of its former colonies in the 1970s, and would thus no longer be responsible for the system of examinations, the idea of a regional arrangement arose. After commissioning a study on prospects for establishing a South Pacific Examinations Board, USP concluded in 1973 that such a step would be premature. During a

Regional Education Seminar of the South Pacific Commission (SPC) at Honiara in 1974, New Zealand offered to adapt its School Certificate exam to better serve the needs of several countries in the region, and B. B. Ramage of the New Zealand Department of Education visited the Cook Islands, Fiji, Niue, Tonga, and Western Samoa for this purpose. Ramage's report was then discussed at the Regional Education Seminar at Tahiti in February 1975.

Favorable response to the Ramage report led SPC to convene a Sub-Regional Special Meeting on Assessment and Guidance at Suva in September 1975, where participants recommended that a new organization, a Board for Educational Co-operation, be set up to develop better assessment procedures for countries of the region. In March 1976, the SPC Regional Education Seminar at Koror, Palau, agreed. When the proposal was further endorsed at the South Pacific Conference in October 1976, the New Zealand government offered to fund a second exploratory study mission to the Ellice Islands (now Tuvalu), Gilbert Islands (now Kiribati), Nauru, New Hebrides (now Vanuatu), and the Solomon Islands. SPC also set aside funds for activities that a new body might initially undertake. Meanwhile, USP discontinued its Psychological Assessment Unit in January 1977, though its new Institute of Education offered to provide some of the services required by a Board for Educational Co-operation.

The report of the study mission by F. Hong Tiy and P. J. Beveridge was discussed in July 1978, by education ministry officials during the Meeting to Discuss the Report on the Possible Establishment of a South Pacific Board for Educational Co-operation, cosponsored by SPC and USP at Suva. As there was a consensus to form a new organization, an Interim Executive Committee for the South Pacific Board for Educational Assessment met at Suva on February 28 and March 1, 1979, and a draft constitution was drawn up and circulated to countries in the region. When the required minimum of seven countries had acceded to the Agreement in 1981, SPBEA began.

The Agreement on the Board for Educational Assessment specifies that the Board is "to assist each country to develop its assessment procedures towards national educational certificates" (Article V). The Annual General Meeting of the South Pacific Board for Educational Assessment is the plenary body (Figure 6.3). The Secretariat is located at Nabua, on the outskirts of Suva. The Secretariat is headed by a Director. Three Professional Officers, an Administrative Officer, a Personal Assistant to the Director, and two supporting staff are the remaining employees.

SPBEA began with seven member countries in 1981 (Table 6.2). Tokelau joined in 1986. Nauru, Niue, and Vanuatu—the three remaining eligible countries—have sent Observers to SPBEA meetings.

Figure 6.3
Organization of the South Pacific Board for Educational Assessment

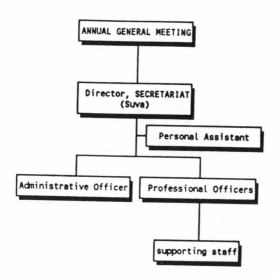

Observer status is conferred upon SPC and USP in the founding Agreement; USP is now considered to be a member of SPBEA. Australia, New Zealand, and the United Kingdom attend as Supporters; they are accorded Observer status in the founding Agreement.

Originally, all SPBEA expenses were expected to be financed largely by the metropolitan powers of the region. Subsequently, the administrative expenses were considered separately from project expenses; the United Kingdom was to defray one-third of the former, leaving the balance of one-sixth for Australia, one-sixth for New Zealand, and one-six to be shared equally among SPBEA members. When SPBEA began, however, the United Kingdom decided to leave the funding entirely to the region, and SPBEA doubled the fractional allocations, which were then reapportioned roughly on the basis of school-age population (Table 6.2).

The draft budget for SPBEA's first year of operation was F$120,000 (US$103,200). The 1987 administrative budget was F$152,000 (US$140,740 before the midyear devaluation). Special project assistance has been received from the British Council, Commonwealth Fund for Technical Co-operation (CFTC), and the UN Development Fund (UNDP) for the UN Educational, Scientific, and Cultural Organization (UNESCO).

The main focus is on the continuing development of proficiency assessment, including in-country consultancy and training as well as training courses in Fiji, adjacent to the Secretariat facilities. The aim

Table 6.2
South Pacific Board for Educational Assessment: Membership and Finances

Year Joined	Participating Countries		Contributions (1987)
	Member Countries	Observers	
1981		Australia	33.3%
	Cook Islands		2.7
	Fiji		5.4
	Kiribati		3.6
		New Zealand	33.3
	Solomon Islands		5.4
	Tonga		5.4
	Tuvalu		2.7
		United Kingdom	0.0
	Western Samoa		5.4
1986	Tokelau		2.7
Totals	8 Members	3 Observers	$140,740

is to develop standardized testing instruments so that member countries will have appropriate measures for deciding whether students will progress at higher educational levels, whether from primary to secondary grades (as in Kiribati), from secondary to precollege curricula (as in the Cook Islands), or from secondary to tertiary education. The earliest projects were the Regional Examiners' Course for educational officers of the region, consulting work for national projects on educational assessment, and consultant visits to countries in the region. A training course in computerized examinations was developed for educational specialists in the region in 1984, and SPBEA is now providing personal computers to the various school systems to disseminate the technology of educational assessment. Classroom assessment by teachers is a current emphasis in technical assistance, as the quality of student preparation is a function of teacher competence. Since New Zealand no longer provides college entrance examinations for the region, SPBEA is now establishing Certificate exams for the major fields of study. Each educational system in the region has somewhat different procedures for channeling students below the university level, so SPBEA develops separate testing instruments for each member country. In a few short years, SPBEA has developed from a central institution to score exams into a major regional certifying board.

In many respects, SPBEA is one of the most basic of all the South Pacific regional organizations. The future of the region depends on how well systems of public instruction operate. The communitarian life of the region, which is manifest at the international level as the Pacific Way, stresses cooperation more than competition and interpersonal harmony more than individual struggle to achieve success. Although SPBEA officially was set up to design objective instruments to determine levels of academic achievement, a testing instrument cannot be designed entirely in the abstract. Educational administrators in the member countries inevitably have called upon SPBEA experts to reflect more broadly on the needs of each country and strategies for improved learning. The result—yet another illustration of the payoffs to be derived from the Pacific Way—has been of more benefit to the region than the official purposes of the organization.

CONCLUSION

Isolated from the development of Confucian learning, the European Enlightment, and John Dewey's theories of progressive education, the cultures of the South Pacific developed indigenous systems of learning appropriate to their needs. The intrusion of the colonial era added little to the educational horizons of the region as a whole, though the leaders who ultimately sought independence found their way to study in educational institutions of the metropolitan powers. Yet independent nations need to provide local training for both leaders and bureaucrats to administer programs of development that will satisfy the basic needs of their peoples. SPBEA arose to assist South Pacific countries in rationalizing their primary and secondary educational systems so that the educational expectations of all can be increased. USP grew out of the realization that the region needed to pool resources in order to provide its next generation of leaders with a new vision. Translating these lofty goals into reality is hardly automatic as soon as a new institution is formed. It is the Pacific Way that has provided not only a glimpse of a new South Pacific but also a modus operandi for moving step by step.

NOTES

1. Basic information may be obtained in University of the South Pacific, *The Report of the Vice-Chancellor of the University of the South Pacific to the University Council* (Suva: University of the South Pacific, annually, 1970–).

2. Basic information may be obtained in South Pacific Commission, *Findings of the Meeting to Discuss the Report on the Possible Establishment of a South Pacific Board for Educational Co-operation: Report of Meeting, Suva, Fiji, 11 and 12 July 1978* (Noumea: South Pacific Commission, July, 1978); South Pacific Board for Educational Assessment, *Annual General Meeting of the South Pacific Board for Educational Assessment: Proceedings* (Suva: South Pacific Board for Educational Assessment, annually, 1981–).

7   TRADE, NOT AID: WE HAVE THE GOODS, SEND THE SHIPS!

INTRODUCTION

South Pacific countries are not situated along major routes of international sea transport. For this reason imports and exports have been less than abundant over the years, resulting in a lack of foreign exchange needed for minimal development projects that one might expect in a newly emerging country. In order to alter these harsh realities, there are two alternatives. One is to produce more goods to attract a higher volume of exports. The other is to charter ships so that trade will be regularized. The two strategies, of course, go hand in hand.

This chapter reviews three organizations, the Pacific Islands Producers' Association (PIPA), the Cook Islands/Niue/New Zealand Joint Shipping Service (JSS), and the Pacific Forum Line (PFL). PIPA's aim was to rationalize production within the region. JSS and PFL provide regular shipping services. Functions of PIPA were absorbed in due course by the South Pacific Bureau for Economic Co-operation (SPEC). JSS, which still exists, inspired the later PFL, a project of the South Pacific Forum (SPF). SPEC and SPF are discussed in the next chapter.

PACIFIC ISLANDS PRODUCERS' ASSOCIATION[1]

In 1964 Ratu Mara, then Fiji Minister for Natural Resources, visited New Zealand to negotiate the price and quota for Fiji bananas with Fruit Distributors Ltd. When he discovered how the company was playing off one island nation of the South Pacific against another to secure the lowest possible price, he decided to visit Western Samoa in early 1965, to discuss the possibility of joint action to protect banana prices. During the South Pacific Conference at Lae in 1965, the delegate from Western Samoa suggested that the South Pacific Commission should look into laws hindering the interchange of island products. Fiji seconded the suggestion. Fiji and Tonga then discussed possibilities of joint action in banana marketing later the same year. Western Samoa next convened a meeting in Apia at the end of 1965, where Fiji, Tonga, and Western Samoa agreed that future cooperation along these lines would be useful. After a second meeting of the group, held at Suva in 1967, the three met again at Nuku'alofa in 1968, where they agreed to establish the Pacific Islands Producers' Secretariat at Suva. In 1968 the name was changed to Pacific Islands Producers' Association.

The organization started informally and operated without a basic charter until June 12, 1970, when the Constitution Establishing the Pacific Islands Producers' Association was adopted during the PIPA Conference held at Suva. Following correspondence concerning changes in the draft Constitution during September 1970, it went into effect on January 14, 1971, when three countries deposited instruments of accession with the PIPA Executive Secretary. PIPA's Constitution was formally terminated at the final meeting of the Conference on March 15, 1974.

According to the Preamble to the Constitution Establishing the Pacific Islands Producers' Association, the basic premise of PIPA was "closer regional economic cooperation as a means of achieving the most efficient utilization of resources and of bettering the condition of the rural populations." Accordingly, the countries agreed "to cooperate with one another in the fields of production and marketing and related activities" for one major purpose: "promoting the interests and economic advancement of rural industries on a mutually advantageous basis for the benefit and prosperity of the producers engaged therein and likewise for the areas of production; and thus contributing towards the promotion of the common welfare and the bringing about of a higher rate of economic and social progress and development of the peoples of the Pacific." The specific aim of the PIPA was "to facilitate consultation, coordination of effort, mutual assistance and understanding, and concerted action in fields of common interest."

PIPA was controlled by the Conference, a series of annual meetings of ministers of trade (Figure 7.1). Meetings of the Conference were closed to the public until 1971, when the Consultative and Advisory Committee was established. The Committee met twice each year and was composed of the heads of government of four countries (Cook Islands, Fiji, Tonga, and Western Samoa) and the leaders of government business of the remaining two countries—Gilbert and Ellice Islands

Figure 7.1
Organization of the Pacific Islands Producers' Association

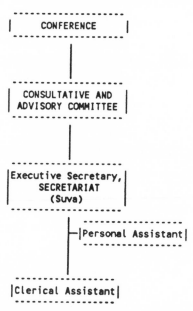

(now Kiribati and Tuvalu) and Niue. The Secretariat, located in Suva, was headed by an Executive Secretary, with support from a personal assistant and a clerical assistant.

At the eighth session of the Conference in 1973, PIPA members agreed to have the South Pacific Bureau for Economic Co-operation absorb the functions of the Secretariat of PIPA. On July 31, 1973, a PIPA Desk was established within SPEC as an interim measure.

The initial conference in 1965 was attended by three countries—Fiji, Tonga, and Western Samoa—with an Observer from the Cook Islands. When the Constitution was open for ratification, the three earliest countries ratified along with the Cook Islands (Table 7.1). Niue and Gilbert and Ellice Islands joined subsequently; the latter were not specifically mentioned as potential members of PIPA in the Constitution, but there was a provision for new members to apply to the Conference for approval.

The salary of the Executive Secretary was paid by the U.K. Ministry of Overseas Development. In 1971 the Conference agreed to a funding formula for expenses of the Secretariat based roughly on the economic resources of the member countries (Table 7.1). In 1971 the budget of the Secretariat was F$8,127 (US$7,006), and by 1973 the estimated expenditures were F$11,030 (US$8,754).

Conceived as a kind of banana-producers cartel, one of the first pro-

Table 7.1
Pacific Islands Producers' Association: Membership and Finances

Year Joined	Member Countries	Contributions (1973)
1965	Fiji	55.0%
	Tonga	12.2
	Western Samoa	20.2
1968	Cook Islands	3.6
1970	Niue	.7
1971	Gilbert and Ellice Islands	8.3
Totals	defunct in 1974	$8,754

posals endorsed by PIPA in 1965 was a survey on marketing prospects for PIPA countries in New Zealand, a study commissioned by the Wellington government. At the 1966 meeting, PIPA countries agreed in principle to a joint marketing approach (though this was never implemented), following the well-established Pacific Way principle that agreements on goals can be separated from agreements on how to reach goals. In 1970 growers and field officers from PIPA countries visited New Zealand to investigate banana delivery and distribution; this led to a study on possibilities of airfreighting PIPA produce to New Zealand and the United States. In 1972 PIPA persuaded Australia to sponsor a tour by PIPA experts of the banana-growing areas of New South Wales and Queensland.

In 1970 PIPA sought membership in the Asian Coconut Community (ACC), an intergovernmental organization headquartered in Jakarta, Indonesia, but the latter responded that it could admit only countries, not other intergovernmental organizations. Western Samoa, in joining ACC in 1971, agreed to represent the interests of PIPA countries. Eventually, other Pacific island countries joined the organization, but not until it was renamed the Asian and Pacific Coconut Community (APCC).

By 1972 the South Pacific Forum agreed to set up SPEC at Suva, realizing that SPEC was to supersede PIPA's Secretariat. Having proved its usefulness, PIPA was generalized to the South Pacific region as a whole.

COOK ISLANDS/NIUE/NEW ZEALAND JOINT SHIPPING SERVICE[2]

The Cook Islands and Niue have been heavily dependent on New Zealand as the main source of essential imports, including foodstuffs

Figure 7.2
Organization of the Cook Islands/Niue/New Zealand Joint Shipping Service

and construction materials, and as the main market for their exports, bananas and pineapples. As the Cook Islands and Niue reached the status of self-governing nations in the mid-1970s, one of the conditions required to make their status more self-sufficient was the establishment of a shipping service on a regular basis. In August 1974, the New Zealand Minister of Island Affairs and the Cook Islands Prime Minister met to draw up interim guidelines for the operation of a shipping line between the Cook Islands, New Zealand, and Niue. From June 18–19, 1975, Transport Ministers and officials from all three countries met at Rarotonga to finalize the arrangement for the Cook Islands/Niue/New Zealand Joint Shipping Service (JSS) in a meeting known as the Cook Islands/Niue/New Zealand Shipping Meeting. The Shipping Corporation of New Zealand (SCONZ), a governmental body, was contracted to operate JSS.

According to the Agreed Report of the Cook Islands/Niue/New Zealand Shipping Meeting of 1975, JSS is premised "on the essentiality of regular and adequate shipping services to ensure the optimum economic development of the three countries" (par. 3), and is set up to "continuously work to improve the quality and economic efficiency of the service" (par. 7). The main legal document, adopted June 18–19, 1975, is known as the Terms of Reference for the Cook Islands/Niue/New Zealand Shipping Committee of Ministers. Terms of Reference for the Cook Islands/Niue/New Zealand Shipping Committee of Officials guides the main working group of the organization (Figure 7.2).

Table 7.2
Cook Islands/Niue/New Zealand Joint Shipping Service: Membership and Finances

Year Joined	Participating Countries	Contribution (1987)
1975	Cook Islands New Zealand Niue	100%
Totals	3 countries	$607,366

The Cook Islands/Niue/New Zealand Shipping Committee of Ministers, composed of ministers of transport, meets for two-day sessions on an annual basis to review matters of general policy, including freight rates, freight priorities, scheduling, wharfage, and stevedoring. The ministers may invite SCONZ representatives and other interested parties. The Cook Islands/Niue/New Zealand Shipping Committee of Officials consists of two senior officials from each country, plus a representative of SCONZ; it meets twice each year to formulate recommendations to the Committee of Ministers. The New Zealand Ministries of Foreign Affairs and of the Treasury consult closely with the Ministry of Transport and the Shipping Corporation of New Zealand in operating the service. SCONZ is required to submit annual reports.

Initially, two ships were involved in JSS. In 1986 the Cook Islands Line, a commercial service, began operations between the Cook Islands, New Zealand, and Niue. One JSS ship was retired, and the other now runs between Auckland, two ports in the Cook Islands, and Tahiti. The service, therefore, no longer serves Niue, which remains on JSS' two organs.

JSS is limited in scope to the three original countries (Table 7.2). Although it is hoped that JSS might become self-supporting, a subsidy for the service is paid by the New Zealand Ministry of the Treasury, based on SCONZ forecasts of costs and revenues. JSS accounts are reviewed regularly by the Audit Office of the New Zealand Ministry of Foreign Affairs, which also contracts with expert consultants to assess all elements bearing on the level of subsidy. The subsidy for 1987–88 was NZ$1,038,596 (US$607,366).

One vessel, as noted above, operates a fortnightly service between the Cook Islands, New Zealand, and Tahiti (profits from the Tahiti run are intended to offset losses involving the Cook Islands). With a view to reducing costs, Avatiu Harbor in the Cook Islands has been upgraded to provide for limited containerization and improved transshipment facilities. Another feature of the service is a discount on freight rates of 30 percent for goods going to New Zealand; in addition, there is a 20 percent discount on freight of bananas and pineapples. In 1982–83, the service carried 38,000 tons of break bulk cargo; most of the load was from New Zealand northward.

JSS well illustrates yet another aspect of the Pacific Way. It was established more at the initiative of New Zealand than because of demands from the smaller Pacific island countries for relief from past neglect. New Zealand benefits by having a steady supply of fresh produce of high quality, while stevedores and other shipping employees and managers have a dependable source of income. Cook Islands and Niue can count on regularities in earnings from their produce to carry out their own development plans, though Niue depends on JSS only in the event that the commercial Cook Islands Line provides unsatisfactory service

PACIFIC FORUM LINE[3]

Smaller Pacific island nations have had one problem in common. They need to import basic supplies and to export primary products through regularized shipping. Although few of the nations have been dependencies of the United States, most shipping in the region until recently involved occasional stopovers at various ports of call en route to or from U.S. ports; freight rates spiralled upward despite the poor service to island peoples so dependent on trade for developmental purposes.

When the South Pacific Forum was established in 1971, one of the ideas discussed at the initial meeting was the possibility of better shipping services provided on a joint basis by countries of the region; this, of course, had been a concern of PIPA, which discussed a regional shipping line at its 1971 meeting. At the second Forum in 1972, the member countries commissioned a study on the formation of a regional shipping line that would go beyond the PIPA initiative, which was based on the economically fragile Tonga Shipping Agency. The study, undertaken by SPEC, called for the creation of a Regional Shipping Council to administer a regional shipping line, and this conclusion was endorsed by the Forum in 1973.

As the Tongan national shipping line was losing money at the time, a Nauruan vessel with a Tongan crew launched a new venture, but the ship, the *Enna G,* was unable to exit from the port of Wellington in 1973, as the New Zealand seaman's union refused to service it, arguing that it did not pay union wages to seamen on board. The New

Zealand government then convened a New Zealand/Pacific Islands Shipping Conference at Waitangi from October 25–27, 1973, with representatives from the union and from the Cook Islands, Fiji, Nauru, Niue, Tonga, and Western Samoa. Although the meeting failed to resolve the issues involved, a Working Party set up by the conference continued to seek terms of a settlement, but the main attention turned to establishing a shipping line that would be broadly regional in scope.

SPEC asked a consulting firm to draw up a proposal for a shipping line; the resulting proposal in 1974 was for a corporation with heavy capital investment and was thus not feasible for the poorer island nations. The Forum again asked SPEC to investigate possibilities. Meanwhile, the South Pacific Regional Shipping Council (SPRSC) was established in 1974 as a subsidiary body of the Forum. SPEC and the Council agreed to a feasibility study funded by the UN Economic and Social Commission for Asia and the Pacific (ESCAP), which recommended a pooling arrangement with the chartering of ships for a regional shipping line. The Forum then agreed to form a Pacific Forum Line on the basis of the ESCAP proposal at its 1976 meeting. A Memorandum of Understanding on the Establishment of the Pacific Forum Line Limited was approved at Nauru by SPRSC on March 3, 1977, then signed by seven governments at Suva on June 16, 1977. Operations began on January 1, 1978.

According to the preamble to the Memorandum, "the importance of shipping services as life lines for the existence of and for the development of the South Pacific region"—plus the needs for "regular shipping services" and "containing escalating freight rates"—justified "the establishment of regular fully rationalized shipping services among ports of the Contracting Parties" through "a viable shipping service with ships owned chartered or subchartered by the Line...."

PFL is a corporate joint venture. As its headquarters were to be set up in Apia, the Council also signed corporate documents on June 16, 1977. PFL reports to SPRSC (Figure 7.3) on an annual basis to establish general policy, and the corporate Board of Directors, which meets a minimum of once per quarter to translate the general policies of the Council into specific terms.

Originally, the Board consisted of a Director from each country contributing a ship to the Line (called a Shipping Member) plus an additional number of members (selected by Regional Shipping Members) so that the total representation of Shipping and Non-Shipping Members would equal seven. In 1981 five countries were specifically named as eligible Directors (Nauru, New Zealand, Papua New Guinea, Tonga, and Western Samoa). In 1986 Fiji was added as a sixth country entitled to a Directorship, with the seventh Director rotating alphabetically among the remaining four members of PFL.

Figure 7.3
Organization of the Pacific Forum Line

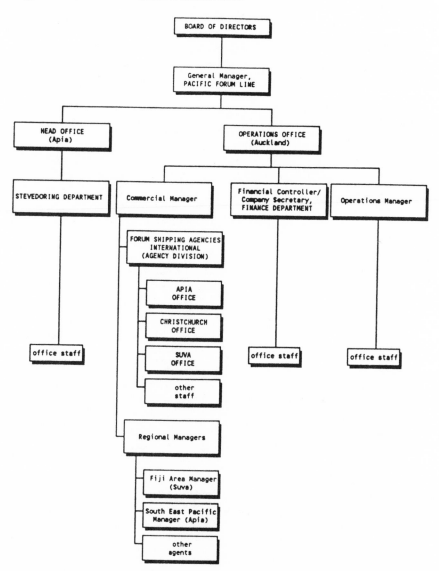

There is an annual General Meeting of corporate shareholders. As five members of SPRSC are not shareholders in PFL, the corporate General Meeting has actual power over the Line. PFL is thus technically both inside and outside the jurisdiction of SPEC and reports to SPRSC as its principal continuing project.

The Board selects a General Manager, who in turn appoints the remaining staff of the Line. The Head Office is at Apia, Western Samoa. In 1980 an Operations Office was established at Auckland, and the General Manager established an office within the Auckland facility. Agents, who are part-time employees under contract with PFL, are available to be contacted in each port of call where the Line operates. There are Regional Trade Managers at Apia and Suva, full-time PFL Shipping Agents at Apia, Christchurch, and Suva, and part-time shipping agents at the various ports of call of the Line.

Tasks are allocated to three persons in Auckland under the direction of the General Manager: the Commercial Manager, the Financial Controller/Company Secretary, and the Operations Manager.

The Commercial Manager coordinates the work of the Regional Managers and Shipping Agents. The Financial Controller/Company Secretary is in charge of the Finance Department, which was in Wellington up to 1984 and is now in Auckland; this department handles accounts and special projects. The Operations Department supervises claims and operations control, equipment control, and the various regional and area offices. The Stevedoring Department is located at Apia, though stevedoring operations are conducted elsewhere as well.

The initial Memorandum of Understanding was signed by all SPRSC governments in 1977 except for Australia; subsequently, Solomon Islands and Tuvalu joined both SPRSC and PFL; the Federated States of Micronesia, Marshall Islands, Niue, and Vanuatu became members of SPRSC but not PFL (Table 7.3). In 1983 the Solomon Islands indicated an intention to withdraw, but it did not dispose of its stock; later the same year, a new government came to power and reconsidered the earlier decision, though there are no PFL services to the country to date. Each PFL member country purchases shares in the corporation. New members must obtain the approval of the South Pacific Forum. Countries that purchase shares of stock in the Corporation are represented at PFL meetings on an equal voting basis.

Originally, Nauru, New Zealand, and Western Samoa were considered Shipping Members, as private companies from these countries signed short-term contracts to start the Line while new vessels were on order. When two new ships arrived in 1979, Tonga became a Shipping Member, and Nauru became a Non-Shipping Member. However, in 1981 the distinction between the two types of membership was removed from PFL's legal documents; representation on the Board of Directors is designated now by name of country alone.

A Regional Shipping Fund, established by SPRSC in 1979, was transferred to PFL in its first year of operations. The initial capitalization of PFL was a subscription of WS$10,000 (about US$5,000) by each country purchasing an equal number of shares. As this amount was insufficient to operate a modern shipping line to service the large South

Table 7.3
Pacific Forum Line: Membership and Finances

Year Joined	Shareholding Countries	Financial Commitments	
		A Shares	B Shares
1977	Cook Islands	WS$10,000	WS$ 54,917
	Fiji	10,000	4,731,359
	Kiribati (joined as Gilbert Islands)	10,000	660,665
	Nauru	10,000	
	New Zealand	10,000	4,318,000
	Papua New Guinea	10,000	5,975,024
	Tonga	10,000	1,199,456
	Western Samoa	10,000	1,480,326
1978	Solomon Islands	10,000	53,930
	Tuvalu (joined as Ellice Islands)	10,000	1,480,326
Totals	10 Shareholders	US$192,308	US$10,376,081

Pacific region, PFL operated at a loss initially while chartering ships on irregular schedules. At a special meeting of Forum countries at New Delhi, India, during September 1980, New Zealand undertook to meet half of the estimated operating losses of PFL if the remaining amount could be covered by other sources. Negotiations then began with the European Investment Bank for a loan to purchase 1,500 containers (leasing up to one-third of its remaining requirements for containers, as needed each year). In 1982 the Forum accepted the proposed loan as well as an increase in capitalization so that PFL could operate its own ships. New Zealand pledged the equivalent of US$6.3 million, and other shareholders subscribed enough to cover the loan (Table 7.3). In 1985 PFL operated at a profit for the first time; it has averaged NZ$1 million (about US$0.5 million) profit each year since then. In the event of a profit, dividends could be paid to shareholding countries, there could be freight rate rebates or reliefs, or a transfer could be made to reserve funds; the latter choice has been made by PFL thus far.

The primary aim of the Line is to bring material necessities to the island nations of the South Pacific, picking up commercial cargo in exchange. PFL charters four ships, each owned by a government or private company located within the member countries. Three ships make voyages that include routes where profits are expected to balance out port calls where losses are customary. One profit-making line operates from Australian ports and two from New Zealand ports, for voyages of three to four weeks. In addition, since late 1982 Australia and New Zealand have subsidized a monthly Feeder Service between Suva, Kiribati, and Tuvalu at a recent cost of US$200,000 annually under the auspices of the Line; the Federated States of Micronesia and Marshall Islands have expressed interest in having this service extended.

Besides providing shipping, PFL maintains its own rolling stock. As noted above, it provides stevedoring operations. Experts at the Auckland office have the responsibility of monitoring trade flows and making projections for future trade patterns.

Between 1978 and 1982 PFL increased its tonnage from 32,583 to 203,952. Before PFL, rates for shipping increased semiannually without an improvement or an expectation of regularity in services. PFL has stabilized routes and reduced freight rates so that Forum island countries have regular access to overseas markets for their exports. In short, PFL has become a success in an area of great concern where the odds were against any such venture—a tribute to the optimistic incrementalism of the Pacific Way.

CONCLUSION

PIPA and JSS came before SPEC and PFL. When discussions ensued regarding how SPEC and PFL might operate in practice, the former two organizations were studied with care. SPEC became a secretariat for short-term projects rather than a bureaucracy saddled with carrying out objectives with an unknown chance of success in the long run. PFL sought to be a profit-making enterprise through a larger set of trade routes that would guarantee sufficient volume.

According to the Agreed Report of the inaugural Shipping Meeting of 1975, the ministers agreed to coordinate JSS with PFL. Such coordination occurs at PFL and South Pacific Regional Shipping Committee meetings by the ministers involved. JSS is similar in some ways to PFL's feeder service linking Fiji, Kiribati, and Tuvalu. However, JSS and PFL are administered quite separately; only the New Zealand Minister of Transport is represented on the plenary organ of both services.

When SPEC superseded PIPA, the Pacific Way of careful incrementalism had clearly won out. PFL's success, in turn, has prompted commercial shipping lines in the region to improve their services in order to stay afloat; one result is that JSS needs to operate only one ship today. As PFL is under the supervision of the South Pacific Regional Shipping Council, a subsidiary body of the Forum, we now turn to a review of the South Pacific Forum, the most important institution of regional cooperation in the South Pacific.

NOTES

1. Basic information may be obtained in Pacific Islands Producers' Association, *Constitution Establishing the Pacific Islands Producers' Association* (Suva: Pacific Islands Producers' Secretariat, 1971); Pacific Islands Producers' Association, *Session of the Pacific Islands Producers, Association: Record of Proceedings* (Suva: Pacific Islands Producers' Secretariat, annually, 1971–1974). See also H. P. Elder, *Pacific Islands Producers' Association* (Suva: Pacific Islands Producers' Secretariat, March, 1971).

2. Basic information may be obtained in Cook Islands/Niue/New Zealand Joint Shipping Service, *Agreed Report of Cook Islands/Niue/New Zealand Joint Shipping Service* (annually, 1975–).

3. Basic information may be obtained in Pacific Forum Line, New Zealand, *Parliamentary Debates, 1979: Supplements* (Wellington, 1979), A. 39; South Pacific Bureau for Economic Co-operation, *Agreed Record of the Fifth Meeting of the South Pacific Regional Shipping Council, 16–17 June 1977, Suva, Fiji* (Suva: South Pacific Bureau for Economic Co-operation, 1977).

8 A NEW AGE IN THE REGION: SOUTH PACIFIC FORUM

SOUTH PACIFIC FORUM[1]

As Fiji approached independence in 1970, Ratu Sir Kamisese Mara, Fiji Prime Minister, realized that the imminent independence for many small island states of the Pacific created international opportunities as well as problems of domestic governance. Regional cooperation, a political pastime in many areas of the world, was an imperative if ever the island countries were to develop modern social environments and economic systems, he felt. Accordingly, he proceeded to explore the idea of a new omnibus regional organization with other leaders in the region with a view to going beyond the more technical and metropolitan-oriented South Pacific Commission (SPC). Preferring to underscore the fact that any such effort would have to be accorded the highest possibility priority, he argued for an annual meeting of heads of government, similar to meetings of Commonwealth heads of government. The Prime Minister of New Zealand not only accepted the idea but agreed to host the first such meeting at Wellington from August 5–7, 1971. A pattern of annual meetings of heads of government among sovereign states in the region was established in this manner, calling itself the South Pacific Forum (SPF) or, more simply, the Forum.

As there is no formal constitution for the organization, no authoritative delineation of aims has ever been formulated for the Forum. The inaugural Forum referred to the advancement of "the spirit of regional cooperation and mutual confidence." The second Forum made reference to the advancement of all the peoples of the region." The third Forum emphasized "the social and economic well-being of the

Figure 8.1
Organization of the South Pacific Forum

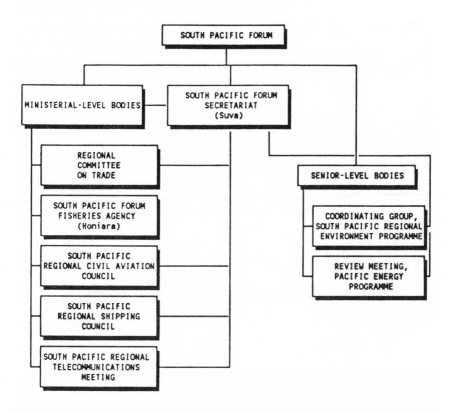

peoples of the member countries...." Subsequent Forum meetings have not specified superordinate goals. Some of the Forum's subsidiary bodies, however, do have specific agreements, as described later in this chapter.

The Forum meets as a committee of the whole. It has been attended primarily by heads of government. The South Pacific Bureau for Economic Co-operation (SPEC), established at Suva by the Forum in 1972, became the official Secretariat for the Forum in 1975 (Figure 8.1). The activities of SPEC, now called the South Pacific Forum Secretariat, are described in the next section of this chapter, as are the various subsidiary bodies relating to civil aviation, fisheries, shipping, telecommunications, and trade. In addition, two bodies composed of senior-level officials have been set up under the aegis of the Forum in cooperation with the South Pacific Commission—the South Pacific Regional Environment Programme (SPREP) Co-ordinating Group in 1979 and the Pacific Energy Programme (PEP) Review Meeting in 1983. SPEC

Table 8.1
South Pacific Forum: Membership

Year Joined	Member Countries
1971	Australia Cook Islands Fiji Nauru New Zealand Tonga Western Samoa
1974	Papua New Guinea
1975	Niue
1977	Kiribati (joined as Gilbert Islands)[a]
1978	Solomon Islands[b] Tuvalu[b]
1980	Vanuatu (joined as New Hebrides)
1986	Federated States of Micronesia[c] Marshall Islands
Totals	15 Members

[a]Observer 1975–76.
[b]Observer 1975–77.
[c]Observer 1981–85.

and SPC rotate secretariat responsibility for these bodies in alternate years. In 1986 heads of state of Papua New Guinea, Solomon Islands, and Vanuatu met briefly just before the Forum; known as the Melanesian Spearhead Group (MSG), their summit was repeated in 1987. This organization, partly within and partly outside the Forum, is discussed in the final section of this chapter along with proposals for a Polynesian Community.

By design, only independent or self-governing states attended the initial Forum in 1971 (Table 8.1). The seven founding members have been joined in recent years by eight new countries. In 1973 the Forum agreed to allow nonsovereign countries as Observers as long as they were "in the period immediately prior to self-government." The Kanak Socialist National Liberation Front (FLNKS) of New Caledonia has not been allowed an Observer seat, however. As Australia and New Zealand differ considerably from the other members of the Forum in economic development, the term Forum Island Countries (FICs) has arisen to refer to the less developed countries as a whole. In 1988 the Forum decided to establish Dialogues with various external funding sources, such as Canada, the European Community (EC), France, Japan, UN agencies, and the United States, immediately after the annual Forum meeting.

Host countries provide facilities for the meetings of the Forum, and delegations pay their own way. In 1971 the Forum established a Regional Disaster Fund; each country was urged to contribute F$5,000 per year (US$3,846 at 1988 exchange rates) to the Fund. Special Forum funds are generally managed by the Secretariat, which also disburses most extraregional aid to Forum projects.

The main business of the Forum is to deliberate on matters of policy, including suggestions and proposals for programs. Some of the policy statements have led to institutional arrangements; others have been matters of continuing concern. The Forum has established the political consensus for several major agreements affecting the South Pacific. The Regional Long Term Sugar Agreement of 1975 sets prices just below the world market rate within specified quotas for member countries, while guaranteeing a specific production goal for Fiji sugar for FICs, though many countries do not use up their quotas and prefer to buy on the world market.[2] In 1977 Forum countries established the Pacific Forum Line (PFL), a corporation examined in the preceding chapter. The South Pacific Regional Trade and Economic Co-operation Agreement (SPARTECA) of 1980 sets up a comprehensive system of trading preferences for FICs to penetrate the markets of Australia and New Zealand; SPARTECA is discussed below in the section on the Regional Committee on Trade. In 1982 several Forum countries adopted the Nauru Agreement Concerning Co-operation in the Management of Fisheries of Common Interest, establishing procedures to regulate fishing within 200-mile exclusive economic zones; this agreement is reviewed in the section below describing the South Pacific Forum Fisheries Agency (SPFFA). The South Pacific Nuclear Free Zone Treaty of 1985 declares one of the largest nuclear free zones in the world; ratified by all Forum countries but Tonga, the more radical MSG countries, and recent Micronesian members, the Prototols have been accepted by China and the Soviet Union, but rejected by France, the United Kingdom, and the United States. The Convention for the Protection of the Natural Resources and Environment of the South Pacific Region of 1986, to which all Forum members and superpowers alike seem likely to subscribe, regulates dumping or storage of nuclear waste, pollution emergencies, and similar practices. SPC is the secretariat for enforcement of this latest treaty.

The Forum has issued declarations over the years on various issues of world politics. French nuclear weapons testing and continued colonization in the South Pacific have come under constant attack.

SOUTH PACIFIC FORUM SECRETARIAT[3]

As mentioned in the previous chapter, in 1967 some of the Pacific island countries joined an organization eventually called the Pacific Islands Producers' Association (PIPA), which established a Secretariat at Suva. When the South Pacific Forum met for the second time, at Canberra from February 23–25, 1972, delegates agreed that a body similar to PIPA's Secretariat was needed to deal with trade and related matters. The South Pacific Bureau for Economic Co-operation was proposed at the third Forum, held at Suva during September 12–14, 1972, when a Director and Deputy Director were appointed. SPEC began work two months later, and the founding Agreement Establishing the South Pacific Bureau for Economic Co-operation was signed at Apia on April 17, 1973, during the next South Pacific Forum. As PIPA still existed, a PIPA Desk was established at SPEC headquarters, only to be abolished when PIPA members terminated the organization the following year. In 1975 the Forum officially designated SPEC to serve as its secretariat. In 1988 SPEC was retitled South Pacific Forum Secretariat.

The SPEC Agreement provides a short statement of purpose: "to facilitate continuing cooperation and consultation between members on trade, economic development, transport, tourism and other related matters" (Article III). SPEC was supervised by the South Pacific Committee for Economic Co-operation, known as the SPEC Committee (Figure 8.2). Each Forum member appointed one representative to serve on the SPEC Committee, which met twice yearly, once just before the meeting of the Forum (the Pre-Forum SPEC Committee Meeting) and once about six months later (the SPEC Committee Budget Session). The Committee now supervises not only SPEC in Suva, but also the South Pacific Trade Commission (SPTC) in Sydney; the latter, established in 1979, is described in the next section of this chapter. The Forum Secretariat provides secretariat facilities for all the Forum's subsidiary bodies except for the South Pacific Forum Fisheries Agency and the Pacific Forum Line (PFL).

The head of the Secretariat is the Director, who in principle serves a term of three years and may serve for an additional term, though in practice the term of office is more flexible. There are about two dozen professional staff and as many general service staff. In the first decade or so of SPEC, under the able leadership of Mahe Tuponuia, the small staff reported immediately to the Director. By the time Henry Naisali took over in 1986, operations had become more technical and there was considerable external funding for particular programs on an autonomous basis. Accordingly, SPEC went through a process of reorganization and became the South Pacific Forum Secretariat. Two

Figure 8.2
Organization of the South Pacific Forum Secretariat

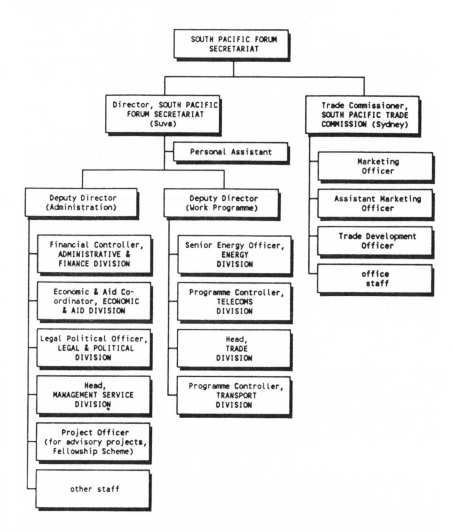

Deputy Directors—one for administration, and the other for the Work Programme—were appointed. Officers were designated for the Administrative & Finance, Economic & Aid, Legal & Political, and Management Service Divisions, along with a Project Officer for special activities and various support staff. The operational staff is now divided into Energy, Telecoms, Trade, and Transport Divisions.

The Secretariat has no membership. Instead, countries became members of the Committee supervising the Secretariat. The seven original members of the Forum signed the SPEC Agreement in 1973, thereby becoming members of the SPEC Committee (Table 8.2). Membership is not limited to sovereign countries but is subject to approval by the Forum. As countries joined the Forum, they signed the SPEC Agreement, though the Federated States of Micronesia was a full member of the SPEC Committee after 1980 while only an Observer at the South Pacific Forum until 1986. As soon as a country is a member of the SPEC Committee, it is automatically entitled to membership on the various subsidiary conferences of the Forum for which SPEC also serves as the secretariat; these bodies are described below.

Secretariat costs are shared in accordance with a formula that allots one-third to Australia, one third to New Zealand, and the other countries share equal amounts of the remaining one-third, subject to "adjustments" that take ability to pay into account (Table 8.2). For 1988 the budget was F$1,393,410 (US$1,071,854). Extrabudgetary funding, which amounted to F$2,558,000 (US$2,114,050) during 1983–84, consists of additional amounts from Australia and New Zealand as well as project contributions from Canada, European countries, Japan, and various international organizations, including the European Economic Community (EEC) and the UN Development Program (UNDP). The Secretariat also manages several special accounts: the Regional Disaster Relief Fund, Fellowship Scheme, Short Term Advisory Services (STAS), and Pacific Regional Advisory Services (PRAS).

The Forum assigns projects to the Secretariat, either on an immediate or a continuing basis. In general, the procedure is to ask the Secreteriat to determine the feasibility of a particular idea, then if the conceptual proposal is deemed satisfactory to the Forum, the Secretariat will proceed to design an implementation strategy, which is again reviewed and approved if found acceptable. The Secretariat's sole arena of concern is technoeconomic.

In 1972 SPEC was asked to carry out "a commodity by commodity and an industry by industry study" to identify areas for export-oriented manufacturing, including problems of tariffs as well as commercial and quarantine regulations. Yet another study commissioned by the Forum was on the conditions under which Fiji, Tonga, and Western Samoa should seek association status with the European Economic Community (EEC). A third study was on the feasibility of a regional shipping line. The first item developed by 1981 into SPARTECA and the Regional Committee on Trade (RCT), which the Secretariat services on a continuing basis. The third item led to the formation in 1974 of the South Pacific Regional Shipping Council (SPRSC). In 1973 the Forum asked SPEC to coordinate action in the field of telecommunications; this led to the establishment of the South Pacific Regional Telecommunications Meeting (SPECTEL).

Table 8.2
South Pacific Forum Secretariat Committee: Membership and Finances

Year Joined	Member Countries	Contributions (1988)
1973	Australia	37.0%
	Cook Islands	1.0
	Fiji	2.4
	Nauru	2.4
	New Zealand	37.0
	Tonga	2.4
	Western Samoa	2.4
1974	Niue	1.0
	Papua New Guinea	2.4
1977	Kiribati (joined as Gilbert Islands)	1.0
1978	Solomon Islands	2.4
	Tuvalu	1.0
1980	Federated States of Micronesia	2.4
	Vanuatu (joined as New Hebrides)	2.4
1987	Marshall Islands	2.4
Totals	15 Members	$919,000

In 1974 SPEC was, in effect, given the power to negotiate with external funding sources on behalf of the region, and it proceeded to draw up a list of private and public aid sources. It then organized an Aid Review Task Force, and the ultimate result was the establishment of three programs. The first is the Fellowship Programme, which began in 1977; one component consists of two academic fellowships per year per country, with funds from Australia, the Commonwealth Fund for Technical Co-operation (CFTC), and New Zealand. The other is on-the-job training in skilled occupations in which FIC personnel are attached to agencies or companies within the Forum member countries for two weeks to three months. Short Term Advisory Services (STAS), which began in 1979, provides opportunities for short-term assignment of consultants from one of the Forum member countries, usually Australia or New Zealand, to one of the FICs. In 1981 the Secretariat was asked to set up the Pacific Regional Advisory Services (PRAS) program, which provides medium-term consultancies to FICs. In 1981 SPEC became the secretariat for annual meetings of the African-Caribbean-Pacific (ACP) Pacific Group Council, a body setup by the EEC to coordinate aid for the South Pacific. In 1974 the Forum asked SPEC to look into problems of news dissemination, and the Pacific Islands News Service (PINS) was founded in late 1974.

In 1975 the Forum asked SPEC to consult with SPC to plan a coordinated regional approach to the problem of environmental management. By 1979 SPEC was coordinating the South Pacific Regional Environmental Programme, along with the SPC, in developing programs to arrest pollution and to protect the environment.

Although regional cooperation in the fields of shipping and civil aviation was discussed during some of the early Forum meetings, and many proposals were prepared by SPEC for action in both fields, it was not until 1975 and 1976 that SPEC served in a secretariat capacity for the South Pacific Regional Shipping Council (SPRSC) and the South Pacific Regional Civil Aviation Council (SPRCAC), respectively. In 1976 the Forum asked SPEC to prepare the steps for a regional fisheries agency, and in 1979 the South Pacific Forum Fisheries Agency was formed.

Energy matters, similarly, have been of concern to the Forum for a long time. SPRCAC, in particular, urged Forum countries to approach oil-exporting countries to obtain some relief from precipitous increases in price. In 1982 SPEC set up an Energy Unit in accordance with the Forum's 1981 decision to give SPEC authority to coordinate regional energy policy. The Pacific Energy Programme is jointly coordinated by SPEC and SPC; the aim is to explore alternative energy sources and conservation programs for economies that seek to be more self-sufficient in supplying their own electricity from sources other than petroleum.

Yet another area of continuing interest to the Forum is tourism. In 1982 SPEC hosted a Regional Tourism Meeting in association with the Pacific Area Travel Association (PATA), and the Tourism Council for the South Pacific (TCSP) was founded the following year. During 1982 the Forum also agreed to have SPEC and SPC jointly organize the first in a series of Regional Conferences of Senior Development Planners. SPEC now provides office space for the TCSP Secretariat.

SOUTH PACIFIC TRADE COMMISSION[4]

One of the urgent needs shared by island countries in the South Pacific is to increase exports. Although SPARTECA is designed to improve access to the markets of Australia and New Zealand, a fundamental problem for countries of the region is to develop marketable exports. In 1979 William McCabe, Australian Trade Commissioner in Fiji, proposed the establishment of an office with that objective in mind. The result is the South Pacific Trade Commission, which operates in downtown Sydney to promote investment in and exports from the island nations of the South Pacific Forum.

SPTC is based on a document called the Exchange of Letters Establishing the South Pacific Trade Commission between SPEC and the Australian High Commission in Suva. SPTC reports each year to the Forum through the SPEC Committee and is headed by a Trade Commissioner (Figure 8.2). There is a Marketing Officer, Assistant Marketing Officer, and a Trade Development Officer; the latter position is a short-term assignment for up to six months, reserved for a person from one of the FICs. In addition, one-month assignments are available to assist in promotional activities. SPTC maintains a showroom attached to its office in Sydney, to display products from island countries.

There is no provision for membership in SPTC. All Forum Island Countries and businesses in the region can take advantage of its services.

The SPEC Committee approves the annual budget, but the Australian government (through the Australian Development Assistance Bureau) provides most funding for SPTC, as the Trade Commissioner is a private-sector employee working under contract from the Ministry of Trade. In addition, SPTC derives income by sponsoring a monthly radio program and through interest on investments. Although other members of the South Pacific Forum could make supplementary contributions, they have not yet done so. Initially, the budget was A$175,000 (US$157,500). The 1986 budget was A$394,000 (US$275,524).

SPTC staff seek trade outlets for entrepreneurs located in the island nations of the South Pacific. This is handled in several ways. Product

displays are one method; exhibitions have been held in Australia (at
the permanent showroom and elsewhere), England, and Germany. Visits to entrepreneurs by individuals and groups of experts render technical assistance so that island products can be developed to satisfy
consumer demands in developed countries. Entrepreneurs, in turn,
visit the Sydney office of SPTC to meet department store buyers, using
office space while they arrange purchases and expand their contacts
with potential buyers. SPTC also locates investors and joint venture
partners for island businesses, illustrating once again the generosity
evoked by the Pacific Way; as Australia volunteered the idea in order
to ensure that SPARTECA would be an economic success. New Zealand
started a similar body, the New Zealand Trade Office, in 1988. Progress,
however, remains slow, awaiting more indigenous entrepreneurship
among the FICs.

SOUTH PACIFIC REGIONAL MEETING ON
TELECOMMUNICATIONS[5]

As telecommunications in many South Pacific island countries have
a long way before the region can talk to itself with ease, the International Telecommunications Union (ITU) sent an expert from the UN
Economic Commission for Asia and the Pacific (ECAFE) in 1969 to
make a preliminary survey of the South Pacific region. At the first
meeting of the South Pacific Forum, the possibility of improved telecommunications for the smaller islands of the region was discussed.
Australia and New Zealand agreed to do a study of the subject for
presentation at a telecommunications conference in Sydney in 1971,
but the conclusions were rather pessimistic. The Union then sent two
experts to do a broader study, and there were two ITU regional training
projects in operation before SPEC began. In 1973 the Forum asked
SPEC to coordinate the various activities relating to telecommunications in the region, and SPEC convened the first South Pacific Regional
Meeting on Telecommunications, known subsequently as SPECTEL,
which Fiji hosted from November 28 to December 5, 1973. Both ministers and technical officials attended, though in due course attendance
consisted primarily of the highest civil servants in Ministries of Telecommunications.

The Communiqué of the Forum in 1974 charged SPEC with four
tasks in convening the initial SPECTEL meeting in 1973: "upgrading
of present telecommunications links," establishing ... "a South Pacific
regional telecommunications network, ... telecommunications training ..., and ... [improved] maritime communications. ... " After about
a half-dozen years of preliminary reviews of the status of regional
telecommunications, SPECTEL made its highest priority improving

rural telecommunications in the region. A comprehensive study of rural telecommunications needs was completed in 1982, and a coordinating effort known as the South Pacific Telecommunications Development Programme (SPTDP) was approved at the inaugural Regional Ministerial Meeting on Telecommunications at Nuku'alofa on April 28 and 29, 1983. The understanding was that SPTDP would be a special project based at SPEC. The ministers reserve their prerogative to meet once again if they wish, though they have not done so.

The resolution recommended by SPECTEL to the Forum in 1983 for the creation of the new SPTDP specifies modestly that the aim of the new program is "a regional cooperative approach to many of the requirements of the South Pacific national telecommunications development...." The SPEC Committee meeting at Canberra during August 1983 declared that a "fundamental objective of the Programme" is "to provide telephone communications to villages in South Pacific countries in order to strengthen economic and social integration of rural and urban sectors." There is no formal document establishing a constitutional basis for the various organizations in the field of telecommunications.

There are three layers of meetings (Figure 8.3). The Regional Ministerial Meeting on Telecommunications is at the top, though it has met only once (in 1983). While retaining SPECTEL, the ministers delegated authority to the South Pacific Telecommunications Development Programme Management Committee to supervise implementation of SPTDP, though SPECTEL and the SPTDP Management Committee are often attended by the same delegates. SPECTEL reviews policy issues, while the latter deals with operations, maintenance, and management, often calling upon experts and funding agency representatives to participate in evaluations of SPDTP operations. The Forum Secretariat Services meetings of all these bodies.

The Office of the Programme Controller, housed in a building on the grounds of SPEC at Suva, implements SPTDP. The Programme Controller is responsible to the participating countries of the Programme Management Group and to the Forum through the Director of the Forum Secretariat. Staff of ITU are provided under the terms of UN Development Program and bilateral funding. SPTDP's Development Project Manager is in charge of consultancy programs and the Training Project Manager ensures that there are competent persons in each country to maintain and operate new and existing telecommunications equipment. (ITU had been funding a training center at Suva since 1975, then merged with SPDTP activities, and is expected to phase out its support in 1989.

Participation in SPECTEL has grown over the years from 11 in 1973 to the present 16 countries (Table 8.3). SPECTEL has some Observers:

Figure 8.3
Organization of the South Pacific Regional Meeting on Telecommunications

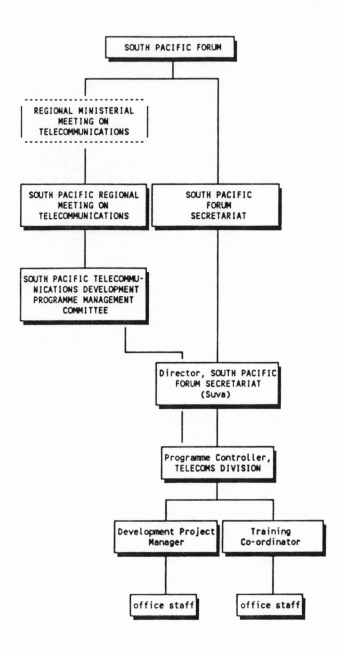

Table 8.3
South Pacific Regional Meeting on Telecommunications: Membership and Finances for the
South Pacific Telecommunications Development Programme

Year Joined	Member Countries	Financial Commitments	
		External	Internal
1973	Australia	$ 209,790	$ 0
	Cook Islands	3,165,000	615,000
	Fiji	29,591,000	1,050,000
	Kiribati (joined as Gilbert Islands)	2,220,000	230,000
	New Zealand	123,762	0
	Papua New Guinea	440,000	53,084,000
	Solomon Islands	8,641,000	1,119,000
	Tonga	2,854,000	156,000
	Tuvalu (joined as Ellice Islands)	1,350,000	0
	Vanuatu (joined as New Hebrides)	4,220,000	660,000
	Western Samoa	10,171,000	747,000
1976	Nauru	3,716,000	400,000
	Niue	1,235,000	115,000
	Federated States of Micronesia	0	0
1982	Tokelau	0	0
1987	Marshall Islands[a]	0	0
Totals	17 Members	$80,036,552	$58,126,000

[a] observer in 1984-86.

American Samoa since 1978, the Trust Territory of the Pacific Islands in 1980, and its successor Palau in 1985. Both SPECTEL and SPTDP have the same membership arrangements.

Although SPTDP is formally a project of the Forum and its personnel are subject to the administrative regulations of the Forum Secretariat, it has more funds than the Secretariat and operates semiautonomously because of its financial independence, though countries pay for the cost of their own attendance at SPECTEL meetings. SPTDP's budget for 1985–87 is A\$106 million (US\$74.1 million), of which about one-third was to be raised by member countries and the rest externally. The amount over the ten-year life of SPTDP is estimated to be US\$300 million. The total commitment for SPTDP during 1986–88 and beyond is estimated to be \$138 million (Table 8.3).

Telecommunications surveys aimed toward an intercountry South Pacific Regional Telecommunications Network were the initial projects encouraged by SPECTEL. These evolved into SPTDP, which focuses primarily today on the intracountry rural telecommunication infrastructure by coordinating national and international efforts. Under the ITU training project, senior technical staff are trained at Suva, and lower-level technical staff receive training at national training centers; 20 technical officers and 30 technicians are trained each year at Suva. In 1979 SPECTEL agreed to a new tariff structure for interisland telecommunications, and by 1988, SPTDP was able to convince the Overseas Telecommunications Commission International (OTCI) of Sydney to provide intracountry telephone calls by satellite at 5 cents per minute, using the demand assignment multiple access (DAMA) system. Access to communication satellites and construction of new hardware in the region are one aspect of SPTDP work, including communication facilities of all sorts (e.g., automatic exchanges, cable and telex exchanges, maritime, power plants, radio, satellite trunk connections, submarine cables, system support, teleprinters, and trunk circuits). Technical assistance trains personnel to use the new facilities; consultancies have covered such sectors as accounting, cable maintenance, coastal radio, legal documentation, and telephone exchanges. In due course all countries are destined to have ground stations with telephone and television reception and transmission capabilities under the new South Pacific Regional and Domestic Satellite System.

SOUTH PACIFIC REGIONAL SHIPPING COUNCIL[6]

Shipping was one of the foremost concerns at the inaugural Forum meeting in 1971. Regional shipping was of concern as well to PIPA; since the Tonga Shipping Agency was operating at a loss, Western Samoa decided to hold a seminar on regional shipping at Apia in 1972.

During 1972 the Forum directed SPEC to develop a plan for the eventual formation of a regional shipping line. SPEC recommended later the same year that ministers responsible for shipping in Forum countries should form a council to develop the idea. A UN study on shipping was also completed in 1972.

However, a Nauruan ship, the *Enna G.* with a nonunion Tongan crew, tried to initiate such a service between Fiji, New Zealand, Tonga, and Western Samoa in 1973, only to find that New Zealand Federation of Labor members refused to service the ship in Wellington. In order to resolve the dispute, New Zealand convened a meeting of heads of government and ministers from the Cook Islands, Fiji, Nauru, Niue, Tonga, and Western Samoa along with the New Zealand Federation of Labor at Waitangi from October 25–27, 1973, to discuss Pacific island shipping and maritime issues. The meeting acknowledged the right of island governments to play a more active role in regional shipping matters, but the dispute remained unresolved. A Working Party was established to continue to explore solutions.

In 1974 the Forum asked SPEC to continue to investigate various possibilities, and a Memorandum of Understanding was drawn up later that year by the Ministerial Meeting on Regional Shipping for the South Pacific Regional Shipping Council (SPRSC). The inaugural meeting of SPRSC convened in 1975. The aims of SPRSC are set forth in the Memorandum of Understanding for the South Pacific Regional Shipping Council of August 28, 1974, principally "to make proposals regarding general policy on regional shipping arrangements and services...."

The Council is the supreme body of the organization (Figure 8.4), consisting of the ministers responsible for shipping in the member countries. The Pacific Forum Line (PFL), which has its own independent structure as described in the previous chapter, reports to the Council each year. There have been two preparatory bodies for Council meetings, which in principle may meet annually. Initially, the Regional Shipping Advisory Board was formed among senior officials in the transport ministries; usually the delegates were permanent secretaries or assistant secretaries, that is, the highest-ranking personnel from the civil service in the transport ministries. The Advisory Board met to resolve problems so that the Council would be able to meet with maximum effectiveness. The first task given to the Advisory Board was to draw up terms of reference for the proposed Pacific Forum Line. When this task was accomplished by 1978, the Advisory Board was superseded in 1979 by the Officials Meeting, which in turn became the Management Group of the South Pacific Maritime Development Programme (SPMDP) in 1986. Although SPRSC established other bodies on an ad hoc basis during its first decade of existence, SPMDP now

Figure 8.4
Organization of the South Pacific Regional Shipping Council

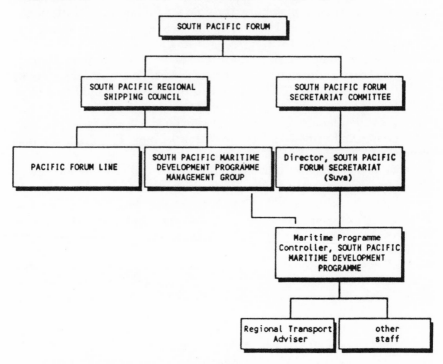

provides a home for various working groups. The Maritime Programme Controller is in charge of SPMDP activities within SPEC, which continues to serve as the Secretariat for the Council.

Initially, Council membership was the same as that of the Forum (Table 8.4). Nine countries attended the first meeting in 1974. Five countries joined in later years. The Marshall Islands, admitted to the Forum in 1986, is eligible for membership in SPRSC. Membership in the Council is identical with SPMDP's Management Board, but five countries in the Council have decided not to take out shares in Pacific Forum Line, the most visible project of SPRSC.

Initially, New Zealand contributed NZ$25,000 (US$20,000) to SPEC to enable work to proceed in developing SPRSC with minimum delay. There is no formal budget for SPRSC. SPMDP is negotiating for UN Development Program (UNDP) funds that have been set aside for regional maritime programs; as soon as these are received, SPMDP will have an autonomy similar to that of SPTDP.

The first success of the Council was the establishment of PFL, which is described in the previous chapter. The Council has discussed other subjects at its annual meetings, including the possibility of establishing

Table 8.4
South Pacific Regional Shipping Council: Membership

Year Joined	Member Countries
1974	Australia
	Cook Islands
	Fiji
	Kiribati (joined as Gilbert Islands)
	Nauru
	New Zealand
	Papua New Guinea
	Tonga
	Western Samoa
1975	Solomon Islands
1977	Niue
1978	Tuvalu (joined as Ellice Islands)
1980	Vanuatu
1986	Federated States of Micronesia[a]
Totals	14 Members

[a]Observer 1982-85.

uniform maritime standards, wage rates and working conditions for seamen, training of maritime personnel, and prospects for future trade and transport in the region. In most cases special committees have been set up to examine the issues and to draw up proposals for action. The concern for future trade and transport led to the Transport Survey of the South Pacific Region, completed in 1984 with funding from several external sources, which in turn led to the SPMDP. Early projects are the drafting of national maritime legislation, including two model agreements—a South Pacific Maritime Code and a South Pacific Seafarers Wage Rates Agreement. Both proposed agreements are still under study. SPMDP helps PFL in assessing maritime needs and seeking funds for supplementary services, including proposals for an extension of PFL routes, fleet modernization, port development, safety standards, and training of maritime personnel. A maritime needs assessment study is underway.

SOUTH PACIFIC REGIONAL CIVIL AVIATION COUNCIL[7]

One of the problems shared by South Pacific countries is a lack of adequate air linkages. Fiji's Air Pacific Airlines began as a step in the

direction of a regional airline, but other nations of the region wanted
national carriers as well, with resulting lack of attention to needs of
the region as a whole. Problems of civil aviation in the region were
discussed at the inaugural meeting of the South Pacific Forum in August 1971. During the following month, South Pacific Air Transport
Council (SPATC) met once again, and the Forum commented that civil
aviation meetings should also be held among island nations at regular
intervals. Nonetheless, SPATC was in the process of winding up its
operations; Fiji gradually assumed responsibility for the various functions of operating Nadi International Airport, and SPATC was dissolved in 1979.

In 1975 the Forum charged SPEC with the task of convening a
consultative body on civil aviation to identify priority areas. SPEC
proceeded to convene a meeting of South Pacific civil aviation ministers
at Nauru from October 28–29, 1975, where the idea of a permanent
advisory council gained acceptance. The inaugural session of the South
Pacific Regional Civil Aviation Council (SPRCAC) subsequently met
at Suva from July 8–9, 1976. SPRCAC has met about once each year
ever since.

Terms of Reference for Advisory Council were adopted at Suva during the initial Council Meeting from July 8–9, 1976. They simply identified regional needs, interairline cooperation, technical cooperation,
and training as the principal tasks for the organization.

Although a conference known as the South Pacific Civil Aviation
Ministers met in 1975, those present decided to form the South Pacific
Regional Civil Aviation Council as the principal body of the organization to hold annual meetings (Figure 8.5). At the first meeting of
the Council in 1976, a body composed of senior officials and airline
companies—the latter represented as observers—was authorized. Originally known as the Regional Civil Aviation Advisory Committee, now
as the Standing Committee of Civil Aviation Officials, the body met
for the first time at Apia from September 22–24, 1976; it serves primarily as a preparatory body for the Council. The South Pacific Forum
Secretariat services SPRCAC.

Ten countries were represented at the 1976 Council meeting (Table
8.5). Subsequently, four additional countries participated. Marshall
Islands is eligible for full membership in SPRCAC since it joined the
Forum in 1986.

There is no separate budget for SPRCAC. The Civil Aviation Survey
of the South Pacific Region, completed in 1985 and funded by the UN
Development Program (UNDP), looked at the main four areas identified by SPRCAC for discussion: requirements for regional air services,
rationalization of existing routes and schedules, removal of impedi-
ments to better services, and training. Although the recommendations

Figure 8.5
Organization of the South Pacific Regional Civil Aviation Council

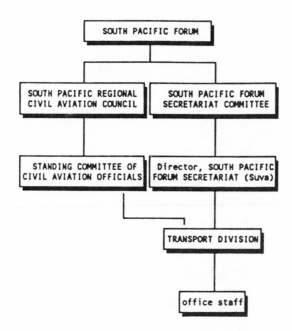

of the study are still under review, especially upgrading of airport facilities, training, and statistics on air traffic, Australia provided A\$ 2.5 million to the Forum Secretariat in 1988 to enable some of the projects to go forward. A regional airline is clearly out of the question. In addition, the Council has discussed such matters as pooling arrangements, joint marketing, tariff reductions, airport security, duty-free allowances, departure taxes, and disaster relief. Since these subjects of necessity involve consultation with the private sector, details have been discussed in more depth at meetings of the Standing Committee.

The Council urged regional airline companies, both governmental and private in ownership, to form an Association of South Pacific Airlines (ASPA), an organization that would be able to implement many of the suggestions from the Council and the Advisory Committee. ASPA was inaugurated in May 1979, but did operate as had been hoped until the UNDP study of 1985, which generated much discussion on ways of improving existing air services.

Since the ministers responsible for civil aviation are the same as those with responsibilities in regard to shipping, SPRCAC has been meeting in recent years at the same venue as SPRSC. Although ICAO decided not to recognize SPRCAC as a regional affiliate, Australia

Table 8.5
South Pacific Regional Civil Aviation Council: Membership

Year Joined	Member Countries
1976	Australia Cook Islands Fiji Kiribati (joined as Gilbert Islands) Nauru New Zealand Papua New Guinea Solomon Islands Tonga Western Samoa
1978	Tuvalu
1979	Niue
1980	Vanuatu
1986	Federated States of Micronesia[a]
Totals	14 Members

[a]Observer in 1982-85.

provides representation for South Pacific countries through its Consulate at Montreal, where ICAO is headquartered. Aviation officials in the South Pacific often attend annual sessions of the ICAO-sponsored Informal Meeting of Directors of Civil Aviation, Asia and the Pacific (DGCA), which discusses technical issues.

SOUTH PACIFIC FORUM FISHERIES AGENCY[8]

For centuries, fishing vessels from populous states in Asia have entered the waters of the South Pacific in search of food from the sea. Fisheries resource management was a concern of the South Pacific Commission for many years. SPC convened several technical fisheries meetings, beginning in the late 1960s, and the South Pacific Fisheries Development Agency was formed in 1970 by SPC in cooperation with the Food and Agriculture Organization of the United Nations (FAO) to determine fisheries resources in the region. In 1973 and 1974, papers by the New Zealand government were presented to the South Pacific Forum on foreign fishing and the need to police fishing grounds in the South Pacific. As negotiations proceeded on the Law of the Sea Treaty in the 1970s, most South Pacific island nations declared 200-mile zones, a practice that may be traced to similar declarations by South American countries fronting the Pacific Ocean. In 1976 the Forum agreed in principle to set up a fisheries agency with the ability to conserve and police the fishing resources of the newly declared zones, then resolved to establish a regional fisheries agency at the Forum meeting at Port Moresby from August 29–31, 1977; the founding communiqué is known as the Port Moresby Declaration. Negotiations then ensued at meetings in 1977 and 1978, but the next Forum in 1978 rejected the resulting draft Convention to establish a hemispheric South Pacific Regional Fisheries Organization, which might complicate its operations by including members from outside the South Pacific, preferring instead a South Pacific Forum Fisheries Agency. Conflicting views led to a compromise, suggested by Australia, that an agency could be set up separately from fishing agreements with countries outside the South Pacific.

Early in 1979, the South Pacific Forum Fisheries Agency Convention was then drawn up; it was adopted and entered into force at the subsequent Forum at Honiara on July 10, 1979. The Convention empowered SPFFA merely to "collect, analyze, evaluate and disseminate" information on the "living marine resources of the region," "management procedures, legislation and agreements adopted by other countries both within and beyond the region," "prices, shipping, processing and marketing of fish and fish products" and then "to provide, on request, . . . technical advice and information, assistance in the development of fisheries policies and negotiations, and assistance in the issue of licenses, the collection of fees or in matters pertaining to surveillance and enforcement . . . " (Article VI).

Nonetheless, the Forum insisted on an agreement with some "teeth," and in 1981 SPF directed SPFFA to explore the feasibility of an agency that would coordinate fisheries research and development programs of all Pacific nations—Forum and non-Forum countries alike. When some distant-water fishing nations (DWFNs) hinted in 1982 that future financial assistance would be linked to an easing of fisheries access, the terms of negotiation of SPFFA hardened. Subsequently, the member countries agreed to a comprehensive arrangement for licensing and surveillance of non-Forum members in the fishing zones of a subset of Forum member countries. This Nauru Agreement Concerning Co-operation in the Management of Fisheries of Common Interest was adopted on February 11, 1982; ratifications were completed by 1983.

The highest organ of SPFFA is the Forum Fisheries Committee (FFC); the Forum Fisheries Agency Secretariat (FFA) carries out decisions of FFC (Figure 8.6). FFC's members consist of representatives

Figure 8.6
Organization of the South Pacific Forum Fisheries Agency

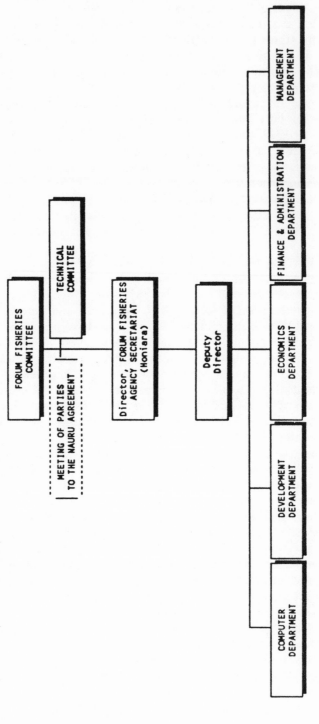

from fisheries ministries and the FFA Director. The Technical Committee, composed of experts from member countries, reviews the work program from time to time.

The Committee selects the FFA Director and Deputy Director. The Director selects the staff, which consists of about ten professional and 14 supporting staff in five Departments (Figure 8.6).

Pursuant to the Nauru Agreement, the Secretariat services the annual Meeting of Parties to the Nauru Agreement. This body reviews the operations of the Agreement but is constitutionally separate from FFC.

Twelve members of the Forum joined SPFFA by signing the founding agreement in 1979 (Table 8.6). In 1980 the Federated States of Micronesia, Marshall Islands, New Hebrides (Vanuatu), and Palau attended as Observers. Subsequently, all four countries were approved as new members by the Forum. The South Pacific Commission has been an Observer since 1980.

Although Chile, France, Japan, the Republic of Korea, the United Kingdom, and the United States were Observers in initial negotiations to set up a fisheries agency with Pacific island nations in 1977–78, in 1978 the South Pacific Forum decided to exclude so-called distant-water fishing nations (DWFNs). The Soviet Union, which concluded one-year fishing access agreements with Kiribati in 1985 and a similar arrangement with Vanuatu in 1986, is categorized as a DWFN, though it was not originally considered for possible membership in a wider fisheries agency. The Nauru Agreement covers seven of the 16 members of SPFFA (Table 8.6); one rationale for having an agreement for a subset of SPFFA members is to try to make the arrangement work in a core area where the most prized fish are found. Then the scope can be extended to other countries to the extent that it is possible to do so.

In 1987 Secretariat expenses were $688,000, with $26,357.29 in capital costs. The contribution formula for expenses of the Agency is similar to the one for SPEC (Table 8.6). In addition, Canada, the Commonwealth Fund for Technical Co-operation (CFTC), the European Development Fund (EDF), the Food and Agriculture Organization of the United Nations (FAO), Japan, the UN Development Program (UNDP), and the UN Center for Transnational Corporations (UNCTC) have provided assistance to the Agency.

Under the Nauru Agreement, fees are assessed in the form of licenses for fishing vessels inside the core area specified in the treaty. Fees are determined through bilateral negotiations between the core country and the distant-water country. Most (85 percent) of the licensing fees are allocated on the basis of where the fish are caught; the remaining 15 percent is shared equally among all countries ratifying the Nauru Agreement.

Table 8.6
South Pacific Forum Fisheries Agency: Membership, Signatories to the Nauru Agreement, and Finances

Year Joined	Member Countries	Signed Nauru Agreement	Contribution (1984)
1979	Australia		37.00%
	Cook Islands		1.18
	Fiji		2.24
	Kiribati	X	1.18
	Nauru	X	1.18
	New Zealand		37.00
	Niue		1.18
	Papua New Guinea	X	2.24
	Solomon Islands	X	2.24
	Tonga		1.18
	Tuvalu		2.24
	Western Samoa		2.24
	Vanuatu[a]		2.24
1981	Federated States of Micronesia[b]	X	2.24
1983			
1986	Palau[c]	X	2.24
1987	Marshall Islands[d]	X	2.24
Totals	16 Members	7 countries	$688,00

[a] observer 1980.
[b] observer 1980–82.
[c] observer 1982–85.
[d] observer 1980–85.

In 1980 SPFFA went beyond its initial mission when it adopted the Regional Research and Development Programme (RRDP), which consists of activities in the following areas: resource assessment (determining the size of fishing stocks), harmonization and coordination of fishing policies among member countries, regional surveillance and enforcement, information services, particularly on market prices of fish, tuna fishing development, economic analyses, identification of fishing patterns, fisheries and administrative training, fishing vessel registry, delineation of fishing zones, and fisheries support services and facilities, the latter consisting largely of miscellaneous activities. Pursuant to RRDP, in 1982 FFA sponsored a harmonization workshop dealing with such subjects as model provisions for fisheries laws; some 50 recommendations from the workshop have been considered for adoption by SPFFA. Other activities, such as workshops on improving fishing technology, are continuing.

Under the Nauru Agreement, a procedure has been established to license all fishing vessels, with priority access provided to regional vessels in the form of discounts on licensing fees. Licenses are granted with certain minimum standard terms and conditions, though they can be negotiated either bilaterally or on a multilateral basis. The Nauru Agreement also authorizes a surveillance program and an arrangement for reciprocal law enforcement. In 1982 SPFFA established the Regional Register for Foreign Fishing Vessels, the only one of its kind in the world, with a uniform vessel identification procedure. Currently some 1,400 foreign ships have registered; only vessels in "good standing" are eligible for licensing renewal. When ten members agree and none disagree, a ship can be designated in "bad standing," and is ineligible to fish in any country of the region. In 1982 minimum standards for entry to Nauru Agreement fishing areas were also adopted, including standard log sheets, with reports on catches and positions to be filed on a regular basis.

If any ship is in possible violation of the Nauru Agreement regulations, FFA is responsible for investigation. Since 1984 Australian ships have been under contract to participate in the Pacific Patrol Boat Project to assist in the enforcement of the Nauru Agreement. FFA purchases satellite photographs to verify compliance. Under the recent agreement between FFA and the United States observers now board each ship every fourth trip.

In March 1982, the U.S.-registered purse seiner *Danica* was seized for fishing illegally inside Papua New Guinea waters. The vessel was released when a fine of PNG$200,000 (US$133,333) was paid. The fine was 5 percent of the assessed value of the ship, the standard fine imposed by the United States for similar violations of its own territorial waters. The American Tuna Boat Association then paid $35 per ton per boat per year for fishing inside Papua New Guinea's 200-mile zone. In 1984 the American purse seiner *Jeanette Diana* was arrested while fishing in the Solomon Islands' 200-mile zone, and the United States sought to apply the embargo provision of the Magnuson Act in retaliation, claiming that the pursuit of highly migratory fish is not subject to the territorial jurisdictions of any state. The Forum, noting the impasse at the August 1984 meeting, expressed the view that a multilateral treaty with the United States might resolve the matter; negotiations along these lines began at Suva in September 1984. In the meantime, the *Jeanette Diana* was released in February 1985, after payment of several fines: SI$12,000 (US$10,435) by the captain of the ship, SI$60,000 (US$52,174) by the company to the court, SI$70,000 (US$60,870) for ship maintenance for the six-month detention, and SI$700,000 (US$608,606) for the sale of the ship. These seizures underscored the determination of the Forum. In November 1986, during the tenth round of talks, the United States agreed on a five-year multilateral tuna treaty. Under the agreement, the U.S. government each year will provide $9 million in cash grants and $1 million for fisheries development projects, while the American Tuna boat Association will pay $1.75 million in fees and $250,000 in technical assistance, for a total of $12 million per year or $60 million over the duration of the treaty. SPFFA's Secretariat will absorb its customary share of 15 percent from the gross fees. SPFFA's Secretariat has also assisted in bilateral negotiations involving Japan and the Republic of Korea. Even so, fishing boats have been caught poaching illegally as recently as 1988.

As programs of SPFFA are related to SPC's Fisheries Programme and the University of the South Pacific (USP) Institute of Marine Resources, both do technical reviews of FFA activities. FFA's Director reports to the South Pacific Forum each year and attends meetings of the Committee supervising the Forum Secretariat.

SPFFA is somewhat unique in the history of South Pacific regional cooperation. As fishing grounds are virtually the only major natural resource possessed by the smaller countries, a strong arrangement was sought so that they might derive badly needed foreign exchange. The Nauru Agreement, difficult as it is to enforce over such a wide area of the deep seas, has enabled countries of the region to flex their muscles collectively against independent-minded tuna boat captains from the United States, who in turn were backed by the U.S. government, thereby incurring the ill will of the region. In the spirit of the Pacific Way, a negotiated solution to the conflict was sought by the Forum, and the result was that Washington agreed to a comprehensive arrangement with the region.

REGIONAL COMMITTEE ON TRADE[9]

The beginnings of the Regional Committee on Trade (RCT) and the South Pacific Regional Trade and Economic Co-operation Agreement (SPARTECA) can perhaps be traced to the nineteenth century, when New Zealand contemplated but ultimately rejected membership in a proposed federation with the six Australian states. The 1944 Australia-New Zealand Agreement, known as the ANZAC pact, included a provision in which the two countries agreed to take steps to consult together to develop mutual trade. In 1966 the New Zealand-Australia Free Trade Agreement (NAFTA) came into effect, involving the addition over time of various items to a list of duty-free products. After 1966, while Australia and New Zealand were evolving a broader economic arrangement, both countries also maintained free trade areas with their colonies in the Pacific. In 1982 NAFTA was ultimately transformed under the Closer Economic Relations Trade Agreement (CERTA).

As former colonies in the South Pacific gained independence, they were concerned that they would lose preferred access to their former metropolitan powers and would be excluded by attention to NAFTA; trade with Australia and New Zealand accounted for about 10 percent of their total exports. In 1968 Fiji, Tonga, and Western Samoa established the Pacific Islands Producers' Association (PIPA) in order to formulate joint action in banana marketing and related issues. Accordingly, the first item discussed on the agenda at the inaugural meeting of the South Pacific Forum in 1971 was trade between island nations and Australia and New Zealand. The Forum resolved that a meeting of senior officials of Australia, the Cook Islands, Fiji, Nauru, New Zealand, Tonga, and Western Samoa should be convened to discuss problems of production and marketing of island exports with a view to establishing an economic union. In the following year, the Forum set up SPEC primarily as a body to deal "with trade and related matters." SPEC continued to do so, and it commissioned a study on trade expansion and economic cooperation by the UN Conference on Trade and Development (UNCTAD), which was completed in 1974.

Meanwhile, when Australia granted independence to Papua New Guinea in 1975, a free trade agreement between the two countries—the Papua New Guinea/Australia Trade and Commercial Relations Agreement (PATCRA)—provided an illustration of what other countries in the region were seeking. In 1976 a SPEC study on bulk purchasing was presented to the Forum, and in 1978 a study on industrialization and trade, prepared by the Commonwealth Secretariat and SPEC, was presented to the Forum. Since the latter report made some recommendations to revise existing trade patterns, the Forum asked the Director of SPEC to convene a meeting of senior trade officials to consider the report and make recommendations concerning greater access of products from island nations to the markets of Australia and New Zealand. The Forum also decided to ask ministers of trade to set up a council to keep trade matters under continuing review. At the same Forum meeting in 1978, Australia announced that it was planning to establish an agency that eventually was called the South Pacific Trade Commission (SPTC). In June 1979, an initial meeting of trade ministers convened at Nuku'alofa, where there was consensus on the need for a trade agreement giving island countries nonreciprocal access to the markets of Australia and New Zealand; the recommendation was accepted by the Forum in 1979. A meeting of the Senior Officials Committee convened at Suva from September 11–13, 1979, and SPARTECA was adopted by the Forum at Tarawa on July 14, 1980; it entered into force on January 1, 1981.

SPARTECA's principal objective is "to accelerate the development of the Forum Island countries" (Article II(b)). The measures to be taken include "duty free and unrestricted access," "the elimination of trade barriers," "growth and expansion of exports of Forum Island countries through the promotion of investment in those countries," "greater penetration by exports from Forum Island countries into the Australian and New Zealand markets," "cooperative marketing and promotion of goods from Forum Island countries," and "commercial, industrial, agricultural and technical cooperation."

The Regional Committee on Trade, meanwhile, has the power "to review the operation" of SPARTECA (Article XI). Annual meetings, which last about three days, report to the Forum. The Forum Secretariat Services RCT (Figure 8.7).

Nine countries attended the inaugural meeting of the Regional Committee on Trade (Table 8.7). Four countries joined by attending later sessions. Delegations include representatives from the private sector as well as senior officials from ministries of trade. Not all Forum members joined SPARTECA at the same time; most signed in 1980, and three countries ratified two years later. Australia did not deposit its formal Instrument of Ratification until 1982, when it had concluded an exchange of letters with Papua New Guinea so that special arrangements under PATCRA would be maintained.

The Agreement identifies Forum Island Countries (FICs) as all signatories except for Australia and New Zealand. The Agreement also identifies smaller FICs, which are to receive special consideration at the discretion of Australia and New Zealand. Although the Agreement does not specify which countries are smaller FICs, Fiji and Papua New Guinea are generally considered among the larger FICs. Nauru delayed

Figure 8.7
Organization of the Regional Committee on Trade

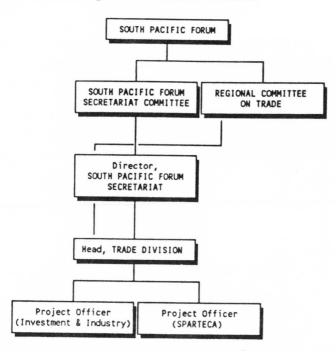

its accession to SPARTECA until it received assurances that it would be classified a "smaller FIC." Since 1985, the Federated States of Micronesia has participated as an Observer.

The main projects, of course, are the arrangements for duty-free or concessional entry of products from FICs to Australia and New Zealand. SPARTECA originally had three appended Schedules. Schedule 1 (3a) consisted of products to enter Australia on a duty-free basis. Schedule 2 (3b) listed products that receive concessional treatment from Australia but were subject either to some duty or to quantitative limits, or both. Schedule 3 (3c) enumerated products that could enter New Zealand, subject to tariffs and licensing requirements.

Under SPARTECA, a product is classified as originating in an FIC if it is a raw product or if the last manufacturing process has been undertaken in a Forum Island Country. All items must qualify as FIC products under SPARTECA's Cumulative Rules of Origin (CRO), which originally meant that a minimum of half of each product must be derived from any individual country or group of FICs. In 1985 the CRO requirement was modified so that entry to Australia need only have up to 25 percent FIC content if there is sufficient New Zealand content to make up the 50 percent requirement; the same CRO applies

Table 8.7
Regional Committee on Trade: Membership and Ratifications of the South Pacific Regional
Trade and Economic Co-operation Agreement (SPARTECA)

Year Joined	Member Countries	Year Ratifying SPARTECA	Contributions (1984)
1979	Australia	1982	$175,439
	Cook Islands	1980	
	Fiji	1980	34,091
	New Zealand	1980	
	Papua New Guinea	1980	
	Solomon Islands	1980	
	Tonga	1980	
	Tuvalu	1980	
	Western Samoa	1980	
1980	Kiribati	1980	
	Niue	1980	
1981	Nauru	1982	
1982	Vanuatu	1982	
Totals	13 Members	13 countries	$209,530

to items entering New Zealand with Australian content added to FIC content.

All three schedules have now been abolished. The Australian Schedules were originally "positive lists," as they listed many products subject to special treatment. The New Zealand list initially had only 11 items and subitems of exclusions, so it was called a "negative list." New Zealand gradually reduced its list to zero exclusions as of January 1, 1988; it has no licensing requirements. In 1985 Australia decided to abandon the complicated listing of items in favor of a negative list of only a few items; these are clothing, footwear, motor vehicles, sugar, iron and steel, and textiles. By 1992 Australia will abolish its negative list, and quotas initially imposed on the items will be abolished by 1996, which will leave licensing requirements as a remaining nontariff barrier. SPARTECA is thus a tribute to the optimistic incrementalism of the Pacific Way.

There are escape provisions for Australia and New Zealand to suspend operation of the Agreement in whole or in part. The procedure is to notify FICs of the proposed action, then within 90 days, Australia and New Zealand must consult with the island countries to try to reach a new multilateral agreement, with the two metropolitan powers reserving the right to take unilateral action. If an emergency arises, the two countries may take immediate action. The Agreement specifically states that none of its provisions are to prejudice any bilateral arrangements between the two metropolitan countries and any of their former colonies, a provision relevant to PATCRA.

As there is no separate SPARTECA office, there is no budget for RCT as such. Secretariat costs are absorbed within the budget of SPEC. Australia provides funds for private-sector representation from FICs at meetings of RCT. Australia, New Zealand, and SPEC also provide funds for specific trade-related projects or assist in seeking external funds for projects relating to SPARTECA. Among the technical assistance projects funded under the aegis of SPARTECA is SPTC at Sydney, discussed earlier in this chapter. A similar New Zealand Trade Office opened at Auckland in 1988. Australia and New Zealand have also provided grants to assist Chambers of Commerce in several FICs. In 1984 the totals of these grants were A$200,000 (US$185,185) and NZ$60,000 (US$34,091), respectively (Table 8.7). Australia and New Zealand have programs for joint ventures and for training of entrepreneurs in their own countries as well as at locations in the metropolitan countries. Trade displays are organized, both by SPTC and by other agencies. Marketing seminars and investment seminars are conducted as well, with funding from the Commonwealth Fund for Technical Co-operation (CFTC) and various UN agencies, with about $500,000 in funds committed in the mid-1980s.

SPEC's Regional Handicraft adviser has undertaken a promotional program for handicrafts. In 1982 SPEC completed an Investigation into the Scope for Closer Economic Co-operation Amongst Island Members of SPEC. SPEC has also developed a Trade Promotion, Advisory Services and Training Project. In 1984 SPEC also completed an Industrial Survey in collaboration with the Asian Development Bank (ADB) and the UN Economic and Social Commission for Asia and the Pacific (ESCAP), identifying possibilities for investment in FICs. SPEC has also undertaken marketing surveys on behalf of FICs for increasing trade to Japan and the United States.

While duty-free entry into SPARTECA has been achieved, entrepreneurship among the FICs continues to lag; intra-FIC trade amounts to less than 2 percent of the total exports from the region, and trade with Australia and New Zealand has risen by only a few percentage points out of total FIC trade volume. The ultimate goal of economic self-sufficiency for the region, depends on how well technical assistance pays off in inspiring local businesses to sprout. An export infrastructure has been provided, thanks to the Pacific Way.

THE MELANESIAN SPEARHEAD GROUP AND BEYOND[10]

In late 1984 the Melanesians of New Caledonia brought attention to their desire for an independent state; several persons were killed in France's effort to maintain control of the colony, which has a substantial percentage of non-Melanesian residents. In 1986 the prime ministers of Papua New Guinea, Solomon Islands, and Vanuatu met together en route to the South Pacific Forum at Rarotonga. As the three Melanesian leaders had often agreed on the need for stronger measures against French colonialism and other matters, including the view that the Nuclear Free Zone Treaty is too weak, they decided to announce the formation of the Melanesian Spearhead Group (MSG).

MSG began only as a caucusing arrangement before a meeting of the Forum, with no formal terms of reference. In 1987 MSG met again, and the three countries proceeded to negotiate Agreed Principles of Cooperation on March 14, 1988, in a ceremony at Port Vila, thereby establishing MSG as an independent South Pacific regional organization.

MSG's agreement is rather vague. No structure is established to complement the annual Summit Conferences. "Economic and technical cooperation, as well as exchanges" are promised (par. 5), but the agreement does not specify an identifiable purpose.

Table 8.8
Melanesian Spearhead Group: Membership

Year Joined	Participating Countries
1986	Papua New Guinea Solomon Islands Vanuatu
Totals	3 Members

When Fiji sought to participate in the negotiations on the economic cooperation agreement in the spring of 1988, the Solomon Islands informed Fiji that the time was not ripe for a broadening of the scope of the organization. Thus, there are three countries in the Melanesian Spearhead Group (Table 8.8). Fiji's native population is believed to be racially part-Melanesian and part-Polynesian, with about half of its citizens of Indian descent. Papua New Guinea, however, has stated that both Fiji and New Caledonia will be eligible to join in due course.

Each country provides finances for its own participation in MSG. The only two activities have been discussions on South Pacific Forum policy and negotiations for the statement of principles. Political concerns override pragmatic issues.

Meanwhile, Gaston Flosse—in his role as France's Secretary of State for Pacific Affairs—mooted the idea of a Polynesian Community in early 1987 at a conference in Papeete attended by representatives from American Samoa and the Cook Islands. In mid-1987, France offered aid to post-coup Fiji, so the public relations effort of France in Polynesia could be viewed as a counterbalance to hostile perceptions of French colonialism among MSG countries. Subsequently, Flosse's idea received support in Niue, Western Samoa, and Tonga (but not Fiji). Tonga's King Taufa'ahau Tupou was particularly pleased with the idea, refining the concept to a nonpolitical Polynesian Economic and Cultural Community that could ultimately include Hawaii, the Maoris of New Zealand, Tokelau, Tuvalu, and Wallace and Futuna, pointing to the possibility of a regional shipping network and transshipment port for Polynesia. When Flosse's party lost the elections in France in 1988, his role was reduced to an opposition party leader while Tonga was taking initiatives to bring the Polynesian Economic and Cultural Community nearer to reality.

The splintering of the unity of the Forum could be viewed as a violation of the spirit of the Pacific Way. Presumably, a Polynesian community, the nascent Association of Pacific Island Legislatures (APIL) of primarily Micronesian countries, and the CERTA countries could go their separate ways. Informal clusters of this sort already existed but had not sought to proclaim their existence too stridently until MSG announced its formation in 1986. The three MSG countries felt that they had been in the minority all too often on Forum policy, so the time had come to assert themselves independently. Leaders of MSG, in turn, welcomed the idea of a Polynesian grouping.

In short, progress on a wide variety of issues, based as it was on a carefully crafted consensus, occurred on some of the more difficult problems in the first two decades of the history of the South Pacific Forum. Since more difficult issues were on the agenda in the 1980s, observers might have expected some impatience in certain quarters. Yet subregionalism may actually strengthen the Forum by providing groupings where more venturesome schemes may be tried, then expanded to other South Pacific countries when they prove workable.

The impact of the Melanesian Spearhead Group on South Pacific regional cooperation could be profound indeed, suggesting that some countries may prefer to defy of the pan-Pacific principle that has been so central to the Pacific Way. So far there appears to be no such possibility. It is an exaggeration to impute separatist motivations in a region dotted by all sorts of specialized institutions for cooperation. In 1988 the Forum endorsed the proposed South Pacific Organisations Coordinating Committee (SPOCC), to be chaired by the Forum Secretariat. SPOCC will include representation from the Committee for Coordination of Joint Prospecting for Mineral Resources in South Pacific Offshore Areas (CCOP/SOPAC), SPFFA, the University of the South Pacific (USP), and possibly the South Pacific Commission (SPC) into a common framework. SPC deferred action until 1989 on whether to accept this arrangement, as SPOCC would place the Noumea-based organization in a role subsidiary to the Forum.

SPOCC may thus be a turning point for regional cooperation in the South Pacific. SPEC has been reorganized as the South Pacific Forum Secretariat. SPECTEL is bringing about inexpensive telephone calls for the region. Shipping and civil aviation programming have taken a new lease on life. SPARTECA has roared ahead. The Pacific Way will remain as a modus operandi no matter what happens in the coming years because the region has learned throughout the years how to avoid being divided and conquered by outside powers.

NOTES

1. Basic information may be obtained in South Pacific Forum Secretariat, *South Pacific Forum: Summary Record* (Suva: South Pacific Forum Secretariat,

annually, 1971–). Yearly Communiqués are published in Australia, Department of Foreign Affairs *Australian Foreign Affairs Record*. See also Gregory E. Fry, "Regionalism and the International Politics of the South Pacific," *Pacific Affairs* LIX (Fall, 1980): 455–84; Uentabo F. Neemia, *Cooperation and Conflict: Costs, Benefits and National Interests in Pacific Regional Cooperation* (Suva: Institute of Pacific Studies, University of the South Pacific, 1986).

2. Negotiations for a regional taro agreement were unsuccessful, however.

3. Basic information may be obtained in South Pacific Forum Secretariat, *Director's Report* (Suva: South Pacific Forum Secretariat, annually, 1973–).

4. Basic information may be obtained in South Pacific Forum Secretariat, *Director's Report*.

5. Basic information may be obtained in South Pacific Forum Secretariat, *South Pacific Regional Meeting on Telecommunication: Agreed Record* (Suva: South Pacific Forum Secretariat, irregular, 1973–).

6. Basic information may be obtained in South Pacific Forum Secretariat, *South Pacific Regional Shipping Council: Agreed Record* (Suva: South Pacific Forum Secretariat, irregular, 1974–).

7. Basic information may be obtained in South Pacific Forum Secretariat, *South Pacific Regional Civil Aviation Council: Agreed Record* (Suva: South Pacific Forum Secretariat, irregular, 1976–).

8. Basic information may be obtained in Australia, Department of Foreign Affairs, *Treaty Series, 1979* (Canberra: Department of Foreign Affairs, Document #16); South Pacific Forum Fisheries Agency, *Report of the Meeting of the Forum Fisheries Committee* (Honiara: Forum Fisheries Secretariat, annually, 1980–).

9. Basic information may be obtained in South Pacific Forum Secretariat, *Regional Committee on Trade: Agreed Record* (Suva: South Pacific Forum Secretariat, annually, 1979–).

10. Basic information may be obtained in Robert Keith-Reid, "Regional Blocs Grow: Melanesian, Polynesian Moves Raise Spectre of Divisions," *Islands Business* (Suva) XIV (February, 1988): 8–9, 38; "Solomons Vetoes Fiji," *Pacific Islands Monthly* LIX (February, 1988): 29; "Why We're Uniting: The Melanesian Bloc View," *Islands Business* (Suva) XIV (April, 1988): 26–29.

9 WHEN HAWAII CALLS, WHO ANSWERS?

IS HAWAII A PART OF THE SOUTH PACIFIC?

The independent Kingdom of Hawaii enjoys the distinction of having avoided colonial rule for most of the nineteenth century, while the island archipelagos of the South Pacific fell under various forms of foreign domination. In 1893, however, U.S. troops from Pearl Harbor, leased to the U.S. armed forces in 1875, supported a coup by a local Caucasian elite, establishing a Republic; in 1898 Congress voted to annex Hawaii. Between 1900 and 1959 Hawaii was a Territory of the United States, a status not unlike the colonial dependence of other island countries in the South Pacific.

In 1917 Alexander Hume Ford formed the Pan-Pacific Union in Honolulu, with the objective of bringing greater unity to the region.[1] During the 1920s, the Union spawned several nongovernmental international organizations in Honolulu, including the Institute for Pacific Relations (IPR) and the Pacific Science Association (PSA). While PSA thrived at its headquarters site of the Bishop Museum, the Union and IPR failed to survive the trauma of World War II and its aftermath in the Pacific. Having been subjected to martial law during the war, the citizens of Hawaii were eager to prove themselves to be good Americans, and the long campaign for statehood was finally successful in 1959, when Hawaii became the fiftieth state of the United States.

Before statehood, Hawaii sought to establish contact with some South Pacific regional organizations, notably the South Pacific Health Service and the South Pacific Commission. The Honolulu-based Commander-in-Chief for the Pacific was the de facto head of military cooperation involving the ANZUS countries. However, during the 1960s, Hawaii's attention was directed more toward the U.S. mainland than toward any other part of the world. Nonetheless, the independence of nearby Western Samoa and Fiji in 1962 and 1970, respectively, served to dramatize the fact that new island nations were emerging, with Hawaii in a strategic geographic role as a hub of commerce and communications between the mainland United States and the newly emerging South Pacific. In due course political figures in Hawaii sought to assert regional leadership, but did so without an intimate knowledge of the developing Pacific Way. Politicians in Hawaii largely ignored the intellectual current of indigenous dark-skinned leaders to the West, while developing greater contacts with light-skinned business executives and government leaders only a few hours away to the East in the new era of jet-set decision making. The story of three Hawaii-based intergovernmental efforts—the Pacific-Asian Congress of Municipalities (PACOM), Pacific Islands Tourism Development Council (PITDC), and the Pacific Islands Conference (PIC)—demonstrates once again the essential role of cultural affinity as a precondition to effective international community building. Hawaii eventually proved to be part of the South Pacific, as we will soon see, when the Pacific Way was accepted as the basis for contact.

PACIFIC-ASIAN CONGRESS OF MUNICIPALITIES[2]

Cities throughout the world are centers of international commerce and cultural relations. Yet formal intergovernmental collaboration between cities generally has to go through governmental channels located in national capitals. The International Union of Local Authorities was set up at the Hague in 1913 to provide a central service point. Since global organizations often ignore the special needs of particular regions, sister city arrangements were established over the years, whereby agreements between pairs of cities have been able to find more specific mutualities of interest. For example, the Japan-American Conference of Mayors and Chambers of Commerce, which meets biennially in Honolulu, demonstrated considerable promise for wider avenues of cooperation from its inception in the 1960s. Accordingly, it occurred to Mayor Frank F. Fasi of Honolulu that an international organization of cities in the Pacific basin could serve to bring together mayors to work together on common problems in an area of the world where intergovernmental regional cooperation had not yet been firmly established. Mayor Fasi traveled to cities in Asia, the Pacific, and Latin America to solicit support for his idea, and from December 1–3, 1971, the Founders' Session of the Pacific-Asian Congress of Municipalities was held, with 81 cities representing 14 countries in attendance.

Figure 9.1
Organization of the Pacific-Asian Congress of Municipalities

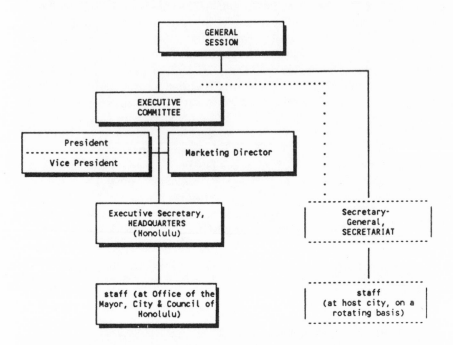

Most of the interest at the first meeting was on laying down parameters for the new organization. Articles of Association and By-Laws of
the Pacific-Asian Congress of Municipalities were adopted, creating a
body for "international research and information for the development
and exchange of ideas, technical assistance and practical experience
in... municipal government" [Article III(1)].

The plenary body of PACOM is the General Session, which occurred
approximately biennially between 1971 and 1981 for three- to six-day
meetings (Figure 9.1). The General Session elects a President, generally agreed to be the mayor hosting the meeting; one or more Vice
Presidents, who serve on the Executive Committee, the principal governing body of the organization, along with the immediate Past President; and one Director from each country represented in the Congress.
Day-to-day work is handled by the Headquarters, established in Honolulu with an Executive Director to handle administrative matters.
Since Directors are often unable to attend annual meetings of the
Executive Committee, officers from the Headquarters in due course
became ex officio members of the Executive Committee and thus ran
the organization. In 1977, in order to ensure broader representation
on the Executive Committee, the position of Vice President was re-

designated as the mayor of the city to host the next General Session. In 1986 the Executive Committee agreed that one of its members would serve as Marketing Director in order to attract new members to PACOM.

In 1980 Mayor Fasi was defeated in his bid for a fourth four-year term. The newly elected Honolulu Mayor, Eileen Anderson, was not interested in PACOM, and Honolulu did not officially attend the 1981 General Session at Kuala Lumpur. Accordingly, the General Session decided to have a Secretary-General as the official of the city scheduled to host the next General Session, in effect replacing the positions of Executive Director and Vice President. A Secretariat was to be set up in each host city, thus superseding the Headquarters in Honolulu that could no longer operate. Former Mayor Fasi, who had been voted "permanent life-long member" of PACOM in 1974, attended the 1981 General Session but objected in vain to the organizational changes. Honolulu's official nonparticipation in PACOM did not permit an orderly transfer of accounts and documents to a new Secretariat. Although the General Session at Kuala Lumpur agreed to meet at Sydney in 1983, the Lord Mayor of Sydney demurred in light of conflicts that had arisen. In early 1984 the Mayor of Kuala Lumpur resigned as Secretary-General, but the Executive Committee did not meet to accept his resignation. The situation improved after Fasi was returned to office as Mayor later in 1984. Efforts to revive PACOM in 1985 resulted in a "revitalization" meeting at Honolulu in January 1986, and then Sydney agreed to host the General Session in May 1986; PACOM was back on track. The floating Secretariat and Secretary-General were rescinded at the 1986 General Session, and the Headquarters was re-established at Honolulu by the end of the year.

The Pacific-Asian region is defined in Article IV (4) of the Articles of Association and By-Laws to consist of the coasts of North, Central, and South America; Australia and New Zealand; islands of the Pacific; the Pacific coast of Asia; and the coastal areas of Southeast Asia and Southern Asia. Any municipality in the Pacific region can join PACOM, provided that it obtains approval from the central government in which it is located.

When PACOM was launched, 14 countries were represented (Table 9.1); the 81 cities were treated as equal members. Over time, the number of countries has varied, with fewer South American and more South Pacific cities present in recent years.[3] In 1986 PACOM agreed to admit business corporations as members, though only five corporations attended the 1988 session in Honolulu.[4]

The representation of Taiwan cities deserves special mention. Delegates from the Republic of China were at the four General Sessions, but some countries in Asia and the Pacific signed agreements with the

Table 9.1
Pacific-Asian Congress of Municipalities: Membership

Year Joined	Participating Countries	Latest Year Participated
1971	Australia	1988
	Canada	1988
	Ecuador	1971
	India	1986
	Indonesia	1971
	Japan	1986
	Mexico	1973
	New Zealand	1988
	Panama	1977
	Peru	1988
	Philippines	1988
	Republic of China	1988
	Republic of Korea	1988
	United States	1988
1973	Bangladesh	1986
	Sri Lanka	1974
1974	Bolivia	1974
	Costa Rica	1974
	Honduras	1974
	Republic of Vietnam	1974
	Thailand	1986
1979	Fiji	1988
	Malaysia	1988
	Papua New Guinea	1988
1981	Brunei	1981
	Singapore	1986
1986	French Polynesia	1988
Totals	27−15=12 countries	

People's Republic of China after the formation of PACOM, precluding any official recognition of Taiwan-based representatives. In 1977 the Philippine Foreign Ministry sought to prevent Taiwan cities from attending in accordance with its agreement with China, but Mayor Fasi persuaded President Ferdinand Marcos to admit Taiwan representatives on the ground that PACOM was a nonpolitical organization of cities, not countries. In 1979 Adelaide pledged that Taiwan cities would be allowed to attend, but the Australian Ministry of Foreign Affairs exercised its authority to interpret its agreement with China to prevent Taiwan delegates from attending; Mayor Fasi then refused to attend the Adelaide meeting. In 1981 the Republic of China was again excluded from the Kuala Lumpur meeting, and Mayor Fasi—attending as the sole delegate from the United States—objected that such exclusion was a violation of the By-Laws of PACOM.

PACOM drew up a contribution schedule at its founding session, with a sliding scale of assessments based on the population of each city, and a flat rate for corporations was established in 1986 equal to that of cities with 1 million or more inhabitants.

The main activity of PACOM occurs at the General Session. Two luncheon speeches, four panels, and three workshops were on the program for 1988, followed by wide-ranging discussions. The theme was "Expanding Municipal Wealth" at the 1988 meeting.

After a decade of operations, Major Fasi felt that PACOM had justified its existence as a worthwhile organization for the interchange of ideas. Although the resources of Honolulu's cadre of urban planning experts was once evisioned as an important resource to provide training for region through PACOM, the economic difficulties of the 1970s precluded such a possibility. Instead, PACOM meetings have served as occasions for an exchange of ideas. PACOM was a first for Hawaii, but the Pacific Way spirit has yet to emerge in view of the diversity of membership from so many continents.

PACIFIC ISLANDS TOURISM DEVELOPMENT COUNCIL[5]

Tourism is one of the few sources of foreign exchange available to island nations in the South Pacific. Accordingly, in 1966 Western Samoa, with assistance from the new office of the UN Development Program (UNDP) at Apia, convened the Heart of Polynesia Tourism Conference. During the conference, Ratu Mara of Fiji proposed an international cooperative effort on tourism promotion among South Pacific island nations. As Fiji was not yet independent, and few island nations were likely to achieve independence for a decade, the idea was not pursued. At the other end of the South Pacific, a nongovernmental Melanesian Tourism Council was formed in 1971 of British Solomon Islands, New Caledonia, New Hebrides (now Vanuatu), and Papua New Guinea, but was abandoned by 1973.

As the State of Hawaii has much in common with American territories in the Pacific, the idea of a special organizational effort among Pacific islands under the American flag led Hawaii's Governor John Burns to propose that Honolulu serve as the site for an intergovernmental organization called the Pacific Islands Development Commission (PIDC) among the territories of the Pacific sending delegates to the National Conference of Governors. Andrew Gerakas, one-time development economist at the UNDP office in Apia and Director of Eco-

nomic Development for Western Samoa during the 1966 tourism conference, was named Executive Director of PIDC in 1972 as one of his
duties at the Hawaii Department of Planning and Economic Development in Honolulu.

Some of PIDC's early projects dealt with tourism promotion. Inas-
much as PIDC saw itself as a catalyst for change with the South Pacific
as a whole, in 1972 it established a Tourism Advisory Council, which
in turn sponsored tourism conferences in 1973, 1974, and 1975, at
Guam, American and Western Samoa, and Saipan, respectively. Accordingly, representatives of the Cook Islands, Fiji, Nauru, Tonga, and
Western Samoa were invited to join PIDC countries at the Cooperative
Tourism Promotion and Transportation Meeting at Suva on October
24, 1975, where the delegates agreed in principle to establish the Pacific
Island Development Commission Tourism Council in a document
known as the Fiji Agreement. As the Agreement specified that the new
effort should begin in early 1976, a meeting convened at Apia from
February 9–11, 1976, where the delegates decided to call the organization, to be operated separately from PIDC, as the Pacific Islands
Tourism Development Council, which existed until mid-1979 and then
collapsed.

The organization was intended to serve as a working base for a
cooperative program in tourism promotion and improved regional air
services. PITDC incorporated as a nonprofit corporation under Hawaii
State law, and a Charter of Incorporation was filed at Honolulu on
August 11, 1976. By-laws of the Pacific Islands Tourism Development
Council were adopted at Nuku'alofa on August 30, 1976. According to
PITDC's By-Laws, the organization sought "to develop through coop-
eration the tourism industries of the Islands of the Pacific and by doing
so seek to improve transportation to and between these island areas"
(Article II).

The plenary body was the Council, which held an annual Membership Meeting one day each year as well as Special Meetings about
twice yearly (Figure 9.2). In 1979 the Council was downgraded in
significance, and the Board of Directors assumed the powers of the
former Membership Meetings. Selected at the Membership Meeting,
the Board controlled its own membership, set policies, and supervised
operational aspects of the organization, which were implemented by
the Executive Director at the Principal Office in Honolulu. Gerakas
was Executive Director throughout; he was appointed by the Council
up to 1979, then by the Board. PITDC cooperated with a consultant at
the Los Angeles office of the Tahiti Visitor's Bureau, referring to the
facility as a "PITDC office," but PITDC never secured sufficient funds
to operate a full-fledged branch office.

Initially, Active Members consisted of the nine governments signing
the Fiji Agreement (Table 9.2). Membership was limited to island coun-

Figure 9.2
Organization of the Pacific Islands Tourism Development Council

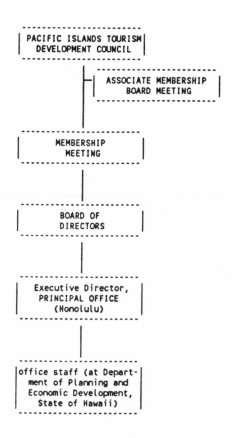

tries in Melanesia, Micronesia, and Polynesia. Invitations were issued at the Suva meeting to encourage membership by New Caledonia, New Hebrides (now Vanuatu), Papua New Guinea, Solomon Islands, and Tahiti. In 1976 the Gilbert Islands (Kiribati) and Ellice Islands (now Tuvalu) were invited as well. By 1978 three additional countries had joined. In 1979 some countries became inactive. The Trust Territory withdrew. Fiji withdrew any pledge of financial support. Tahiti, though it did not withdraw, never provided any financial support to PITDC.

The Suva meeting issued invitations to airlines operating in the South Pacific to become members of PITDC. Although these business firms declined, volunteer professionals in the field of tourism were informally considered to be associate members. An Associate Membership Board Meeting (until 1977 called the Advisory Board), convened in 1977, 1978, and 1979. Delegates at both of these bodies formulated policy alternatives for consideration by the Council and

Table 9.2
Pacific Islands Tourism Development Council: Membership and Finances

Year Joined	Member Countries	Contribution (1978)
1975	American Samoa	$11,000
	Cook Islands	11,000
	Fiji	11,000[a]
	Guam	11,000
	Hawaii	11,000[b]
	Nauru	11,000
	Tonga	11,000
	Trust Territory of the Pacific Islands (withdrew 1979)	11,000
	Western Samoa	11,000
1976	Papua New Guinea	11,000
	Tahiti	11,000[a]
1978	Northern Mariana Islands	11,000
Totals	12-12=0 Members	$58,288[c]

[a]Unpaid.
[b]Excluding donated office facilities and staff.
[c]The total is the sum of actual expenditures, not pledges. When the organization was dissolved in 1981, $64,863.22 was unspent.

Board of Directors. Associate Members paid annual $100 fees to attend the Associate Membership Board Meeting. Equal contributions were to be paid by Active Members (Table 9.2).

At the time of the dissolution of PITDC, $64,863.22 was in the bank account of the organization, including interest that had accrued since the latest contribution. The successor organization, the Pacific Basic Development Commission (PBDC), decided to return this amount to each member in the exact percentage of the proportions contributed by the members during the existence of PITDC.

Projects of PITDC closely followed the statement of functions outlined in the Fiji Agreement. A promotional brochure on South Pacific tourism was prepared in conjunction with group tours to the region— the first major cooperative multicountry tourist project for the South Pacific. In addition, PITDC adopted a marketing program, including preparation of a slide show, agent's manual, appearance at trade shows, and an advertising and publicity campaign. PITDC also lobbied for the establishment of more air transportation among the island countries.

Yet these efforts assumed that tourist facilities in the Pacific island countries were adequate, that potential tourists to the region could easily be identified, and that there was no competition among the various island tourist destinations. All three assumptions were, of course, incorrect. Many exotic ports of call even today lack facilities required by tourists accustomed to lavish accommodations. Basic research to identify scuba divers, white water rafters, and potential tourists with other interests has lagged. Fiji, Hawaii, and Tahiti continue to compete with each other, and air routes make Fiji a point of entry to many other parts of the South Pacific, so advertising may only serve to perpetuate the current pattern of tourist spending in the region. PITDC was perceived, albeit perhaps incorrectly, as an initiative that would bring disproportionate benefit to Hawaii. Lacking sufficient funding, PITDC was primarily a paper organization and was unable to go beyond the limitations of its initially determined scope.

As noted above, PITDC was created by the Pacific Islands Development Commission (PIDC), which also set up the Pacific Tuna Development Foundation (PTDF) in 1974. All three were headquartered in Honolulu, though only PITDC included governments of jurisdictions outside the United States and its associated states. When the Trust Territory of the Pacific Islands split in 1980 into entities now known as the Federated States of Micronesia, Marshall Islands, Northern Mariana Islands, and Palau, PIDC was considered obsolete. Accordingly, in 1980 a new organization, the Pacific Basin Development Council (PBDC), superseded PIDC, with American Samoa, Guam, Hawaii, and the Commonwealth of Northern Mariana Islands as members. As PITDC was moribund at the time of PBDC's formation, the latter recommended dissolution of PITDC, an event that took place in 1981. In 1985 PTDF was superseded by the Pacific Fisheries Development Foundation (PFDF), which had been reorganized on a nongovernmental basis in 1980, with the same membership as PBDC plus the Federated States of Micronesia, Marshall Islands, and Palau.

Hawaii's second intergovernmental initiative in the region focused its attention entirely on the newly emerging island nations. However, the South Pacific Forum already existed, and the South Pacific Bureau for Economic Co-operation (SPEC) had been asked to look into problems of tourist promotion. Although a SPEC representative presented a report to PITDC in 1977, the interests of the two organizations differed. The Pacific Way was growing in Suva but was still largely unknown in Honolulu. Efforts by SPEC eventually resulted in the formation of the Tourism Council of the South Pacific (TCSP), described later in this volume, where directors of government visitors' bureaus have a larger role to play than PITDC, which was more oriented toward the immediate needs of the private sector.

PACIFIC ISLANDS CONFERENCE[6]

The Center for Cultural Interchange Between East and West, known as the East-West Center, was established by Congress and opened in 1960 by the U.S. Department of State on the campus of the University of Hawaii. The Center in due course became famous for supporting students at the University, holding conferences on a variety of topics, and providing funds for scholars to complete research. In 1975 the institution became an independent nonprofit corporation under Hawaii law with a change in name to the Center for Cultural and Technical Interchange Between East and West, Inc. Since the Center then considered itself answerable to several countries in the Asia-Pacific region, the Board of Directors of the new corporation provided a wide multinational representation. Fiji's Ratu Mara, for example, was a charter member of the Board.

Previously organized into institutes and programs in functional areas, Everett Kleinjans as first President thought that a special institute should be established to deal with the island nations of the Pacific. Consulting with Ratu Mara, Tonga's S. Langi Kavaliku, and officials at the South Pacific Bureau for Economic Co-operation (SPEC) and the South Pacific Commission (SPC), he was encouraged to proceed, as Hawaii was deemed to a place where leaders from the region would be more free to talk. Several persons indeed suggested that the Center convene a meeting of key government officials from the South Pacific, who in turn could assist the Center in formulating a work program for an institute relevant to the needs of the newly emerging Pacific islands. At that point the Pacific Way took over. A Pre-Conference Planning Meeting convened at the East-West Center from October 29 to November 2, 1979, and the First Pacific Islands Conference met at the East-West Center, Honolulu, from March 26–29, 1980. It was at this meeting that the Center's Pacific Islands Development Program (PIDP) was launched. In 1985, when the Second Pacific Islands Conference convened, the framework for the organization was firmly established and the scope was in effect widened from a determination of PIDP priorities to a concern for problems of development within the South Pacific island nations in general.

No charter was adopted for the Conference, which meets on an informal basis. The Concluding Statement of the first Conference specified that the essence of PIC was "to identify priority areas where governmental, regional, and/or international action and research and training programs are required to establish national and regional strategies to meet both immediate and long-term goals."

The Pacific Islands Conference, therefore is basically a meeting of heads of governments and administrations of Pacific countries (Figure

Figure 9.3
Organization of the Pacific Islands Conference

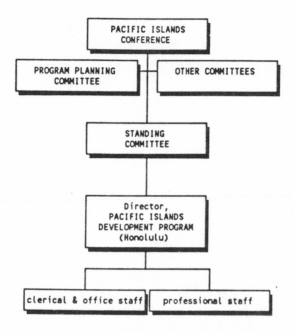

9.3). Papers are read by the government leaders, then committees on specialized subjects draw up priority areas for attention, followed by an approval of committee reports at the final plenary session. The committees are concerned with the following types of subjects: goals and development strategies for the Pacific islands as a whole, the Pacific islands in the world community, regional cooperation, administrative and government structures appropriate to Pacific islands development, cultural development and conservation, and energy needs.

The inaugural Conference then established the Program Planning Committee, composed of senior officials of Pacific island countries, to identify specific projects in the areas of priority determined by the Conference; this body meets about once every two years. To review the work of PIDP on a more regular basis, a smaller Standing Committee was established to meet at six-month intervals; the third to fifth meetings were teleconferences over a communication satellite, known as PEACESAT, operated by the University of Hawaii. Membership on the Standing Committee originally consisted of heads of government of six island countries, with a Secretary-General at the level of minister from a seventh island country; the number was increased in 1981 (Table 9.3). The first Chairman of the Program Planning Committee

Table 9.3
Pacific Islands Conference: Membership in the Conference, Program Planning Committee (PPC), and Standing Committee (SC), and Financial Contributions

Year Joined	Participating Countries	PPC	SC	Contribution (1981-84)
1980	American Samoa	1980	1980[c]	$ 2,000
	Australia (withdrew 1986)			155,149
	Canada			
	Cook Islands	1980	1980	4,000
	Fiji	1980	1980	20,000
	French Polynesia		1980[d]	
	Guam[a]		1980[c]	
	Hawaii	1980	1981[e]	100,000
	Japan		1987	320,000
	Kiribati		1980[f]	6,000
	Marshall Islands			5,000
	Nauru			
	New Caledonia		1980[d]	
	New Zealand			16,689
	Northern Mariana Islands		1980[c]	
	Palau (joined as Trust Territory of the Pacific Islands)			
	Papua New Guinea	1980	1980	47,663
	Solomon Islands[a]			
	Tonga	1980	1980	11,224
	Tuvalu			
	United Kingdom			
	Vanuatu (joined as New Hebrides)[a]			
	Western Samoa	1980		
1985	Chile			
	Federated States of Micronesia		1981	12,000
	Niue			
	Tokelau[b]			
Totals	**27-4=23 countries**	**8**	**8**	**$699,725**

[a]Represented by the Pacific Basin Development Commission.
[b]Represented by the Vice President, Conseil du Gouvernment, French Pacific Territories.
[c]Originally represented by the Pacific Basic Development Commission; now has a seat of its own.
[d]Seat expired in 1987.
[e]Not at the 1985 Conference.
[f]Considered a member, though it has not attended any meetings thus far.

became the Secretary-General of the Standing Committee. PIDP was designated as responsible for the functions of an informal secretariat for future meetings. PIDP's Director thus serves as the chief administrative officer for PIC. There is no formal membership requirement to attend meetings of the Conference, which purports to represent the interests of all countries of the region (Table 9.3). The first Conference was attended by representatives from 23 countries. In addition, there were observers from various organizations, both governmental and nongovernmental. Attendance increased at the second Conference, held in 1985, to include Chile, the Federated States of Micronesia, and

Niue, but Australia decided to withdraw in 1986. Tokelau is considered to be a member country, though it has not yet sent any representatives to PIC meetings.

Since the Standing Committee was designed as a smaller working group, certain key countries were given seats by the Conference, including a position for the Vice President, Counseil du Gouvernment, for all French Pacific territories, and a representative of the Pacific Basic Development Commission on behalf of all U.S.-flag territories. As PIDP is in Hawaii, Standing Committee membership expanded in 1981 to include a permanent position for Hawaii, and a rotating seat was assigned to the other three U.S.-flag countries in the Pacific. The President of the Federated States of Micronesia was also invited to join in 1981. In 1987 Japan's Consul-General in Honolulu attended as a governmental representative, with the U.S. Agency for International Development (USAID) as an observer.

The East-West Center provided most of the funding for the initial meeting. Host governments provide conference facilities; expenses of participation are borne by each government attending. PIDP operates on an annual budget of about $370,000, based on voluntary contributions (Table 9.3). There are four professional and six administrative personnel in all. PIDP projects are funded on a project-by-project basis from several external sources, including the International Labor Organization (ILO), SPC, SPEC, and the UN Development Program (UNDP), which attend PIC as observers.

Projects identified at the first Conference were in the fields of appropriate government systems for development, aquaculture, disaster preparedness, energy, faculty development, indigenous business development, nuclear waste disposal, regional cooperation, and the role of multinational corporations in development of Pacific island countries. All projects involve studies and conferences, responding to specific questions posed in terms of reference for each project set forth by the Standing Committee. Progress reports and final reports contain answers to questions and related policy recommendations, which are forwarded to the Standing Committee.

The second Conference agreed to continue five projects (in the fields of disaster preparedness, energy, government and administrative systems, indigenous business development, and faculty development). The multinational corporations project was continued as two projects, one focusing on the tuna industry, the other on petroleum marketing and supply. Five new projects were authorized in the fields of health and nutrition, policy analysis (which aims to build a data bank about Pacific island nations), a study of the role of the private sector in development, urban migration and rural life, and a project on the problems of and employment opportunities for youth. Currently, PIDP engages in integrated projects, combining research with training of management personnel in the fields of public policy analysis and tourism.

As PIDP activities appear to overlap with the South Pacific Bureau for Economic Co-operation (SPEC) and the South Pacific Commission (SPC), both organizations were involved in the original Pre-Conference Planning Committee, and they have been represented at later Conference sessions. In 1985 SPEC was accorded the role of Observer at meetings of the Standing Committee. The same status was granted to the Committee for Co-ordination of Joint Prospecting for Mineral Resources in South Pacific Offshore Areas (CCOP/SOPAC) in 1987.

Some projects have been undertaken in collaboration and consultation with other international organizations in the region. The environmental project involves consultation with the South Pacific Commission. Unlike other institutes of the East-West Center, PIDP undertakes no projects without explicit PIC authorization. In practice, this means that the PIDP Director, a scholar from the South Pacific, proposes a work program, which in turn is subject to review and modification by the heads of government. PIDP is carefully insulated from U.S. government control, though no institution in the South Pacific or elsewhere can claim to be free from the priorities of its funding sources.

A question, therefore, arises as to why PIDP is allowed to exist alongside SPEC and SPC, or why funds go to PIDP rather than strengthening the University of the South Pacific (USP). Clearly, leaders of the Pacific island nations have several reasons in mind. SPC continues to be useful in the areas where it operates, but there is a reluctance to give it new tasks, since it is perceived as ossified. The South Pacific Forum Secretariat is set up for immediate implementation of decisions by the Forum, so it is not designed for broader surveys on possibilities and resources. USP, meanwhile, rivals the University of Papua New Guinea in seeking to develop both a more indigenous teaching faculty and a more internationally distinguished reputation for excellence. The East-West Center, in contrast, can not only draw upon expertise from well-recognized faculty at the University of Hawaii in many fields of study, but also can readily attract notable scholars from the region and elsewhere to work at PIDP. Japan and the United States are more willing to assist PIDP than USP. PIC, therefore, exists to guide PIDP as a "think tank" for the South Pacific. The origin of PIC as a product of Pacific Way consultations guarantees its continued success.

CONCLUSION

Three initiatives in regional cooperation from various quarters in Hawaii were tried in the last two decades. The Honolulu Mayor's ambitious goal was to develop a hemispheric body, headquartered in Honolulu, for mayors of cities from three continents and South Pacific islands to discuss problems of running cities. The Governor of Hawaii supported an organization to promote tourism for Pacific island destinations. The President of the East-West Center began an effort that eventually resulted in a think tank under the control of South Pacific leaders.

PACOM ran aground in the early 1980s because of the vastness of the region, the economic troubles of the times, the defeat of the prime mover in an election, and squabbles regarding the foreign policy commitments of sovereign states in regard to an outdated "two China" policy. When PACOM rebounded in 1986, it returned to a low-key role as a three-day conference of mayors and supportive corporations. PITDC was regarded with jealousy by Fiji and Tahiti, sensing that the Pacific Way was not the modus operandi, and a separate tourist promotion organization was later set up among Pacific island countries. Although some observers might find something sinister in having a South Pacific regional organization headquartered in a U.S. city,[7] they are perhaps unaware of the extent to which Honolulu is ignored by policymakers in Washington; a Third World orientation pervades the culture, and leaders and people alike yearn for an independent role as a unique multiracial society in the Pacific. PIC has proved to be more successful than PACOM and PITDC because countries of the South Pacific have been in the driver's seat from the start. South Pacific islanders direct and implement the work of PIDP. Hawaii could not intrude itself into a role of leadership in the region on its own terms; instead, through PIC Hawaii was adopted, so to speak, by the South Pacific as an important contributor to the region. The Pacific Way once again proved to be the most dynamic source of regional cooperation for the South Pacific.

NOTES

1. For more information on early efforts to build a Pacific community in Hawaii, see Michael Haas and George S. Kanahele, "Prospects for Pacific Community," *Pacific Community* (Tokyo) VI (October, 1974): 83–93; Paul F. Hooper, "A History of Internationalism in Hawaii Between 1900 and 1940" (Ph.D. diss.: University of Hawaii, 1972).

2. Basic information may be obtained in Pacific-Asian Congress of Municipalities, *Articles of Association and By-Laws* (Honolulu: Pacific-Asian Congress of Municipalities, 1971, 1973, 1977; Kuala Lumpur: Pacific-Asian Congress of Municipalities, 1981); Pacific-Asian Congress of Municipalities, *International Cooperation for Better Government: Founders' Session, Honolulu, Hawaii, December 1–3, 1971* (Honolulu: Pacific-Asian Congress of Municipal-

ities, 1971); Pacific-Asian Congress of Muncipalities, *Conference Proceedings: General Session* (1974, 1975, 1977, 1979, 1981, 1986, 1988).

3. Cities represented are as follows. From *Australia*: Adelaide, Albany, Albert, Albury, Alice Springs, Altona, Arapiles, Avon, Bairnsale, Balranald, Barossa, Belmont, Berwick, Blacktown, Blue Mountains, Botany, Box Hill, Brighton, Brisbane, Broadmeadows, Brunswick, Cabonne, Cairns, Camberwell, Canberra, Clare, Cohuna, Croydon, Doncastore & Templeston, Dudley, East Loddon, Enfield, Eurobodalla, Frankston, Fremantle, Geelong, Glenelg, Gold Coast, Gosnell, Hamilton, Heidelberg, Henley & Grange, Hindmarsh, Ipswich, Kadina, Kensington & Norwood, Launceston, Light, Lilydale, Marion, Maryborough, Meadows, Melbourne, Melton, Mildura, Millicent, Minlaton, Moe, Moonta, Moorabbin, Moree Plains, Morwell, Mt. Gambier, Mt. Isa, Munno Para, Murray Bridge, Naracoorte, Newcastle, Noarlunga, North Sydney, Northam, Oxley, Pamerston, Parramatta, Payneham, Perth, Peterborough, Pine Rivers, Pinnaroo, Pioneer, Port Elliot & Goolwa, Port Pirie, Prospect, Ringwood, Rundle, Ryde, St. Peters, Salisbury, Sandringham, Shellharbour, South Melbourne, Stanthorpe, Sterling, Swan, Sydney, Tamworth, Tee Tree Gully, Templestowe, Toowoomba, Townsville, Unley, Victor Harbour, Walkerville, Wanneroo, Waverly, Werribee, West Torrens, Whyalla, Wodonga, Wollongong, Wongan-Ballida, Woodville, Worringah. From *Bangladesh*: Dhaka. From *Bolivia*: La Paz. From *Brunei*: Bandar Seri Bagawan. From *Canada*: Calgary, Ottawa, Vancouver, West Vancouver. From *Ecuador*: Quito. From *Fiji*: Ba, Ha, Labasa, Lami, Lautoka, Lautori, Nadi, Nausori, Sigatoka, Suva. From *French Polynesia*: Papeete, Punaauia. From *Honduras*: Tegucigalpa. From *India*: Bangalore, Bombay, Lucknow, Madurai, Trivandrum. From *Indonesia*: Bogor, Kutamadya Udjung Pandang, Makassar, Semarang, Surabaya, Suribayada. From *Japan*: Fuji Yochida, Ginowan, Kashiwa, Kawaguchi, Naha, Nemoto, Nirazaki, Sakaide. Japan. From *Malaysia*: Ipoh, Kelang, Kota Bahru, Kota Minabalu, Kota Setar, Kuala Lumpur, Malacca, Pahang, Penang. From *Mexico*: Colima, Guadalajara. From *New Zealand*: Auckland, Lower Hutt, Manukau, Waitemata. From *Panama*: Chitre, David, Las Minas, Ocu, Panama City, Pese, Puerto Armuelles, San Miguelito, Santiago. From *Papua New Guinea*: Port Moresby, Rabaul. From *Peru*: Chaclacayo, Lima, Miraflores, San Isidro, Santa Maria del Mar. From the *Philippines*: Aparri Cagayam, Bagatsing, Basilan, Batac, Bongabong, Bulacan, Calamba, Caloocan, Canda, Capiz, Carmen City, Catubig, Cotabato, Currimao, Dandara, Dagupan, Dapitan, Davao, Gasan, Iloilo, Koronadal, Lesgaspi, Llanera, Lucena, Makati, Malolos, Maluso Masilan, Manila, Marawi City, Maria Aurora, Marikina, Misamis Oriental, Muntinlupa, Navotas, Negros Occidental, Paranaque, Pateros, Pontevedra, Pulilan, Quezon City, Sagay, San Carlos, San Fabian, San Jose, San Juan, Tanavan, Tangub, Toledo City. From the *Republic of China*: Chia, Hwalien, Kaoshiung, Keelung, Nantou, Taichung, Tainan, Taipei, Taoyuen. From the *Republic of Korea*: Ahsan, Andong, Cheju, Cheongju, Chunahn, Chuncheon, Chungju, Geoje, Inchon, Hwasung, Junju, Kwangju, Kyong Gi Do, Kyongju, Masan, Paju, Pusan, Seoul, Suwon, Taegu, Taejon, Ulsan, Umsung, Wonju, and Yongin. From the *Republic of Vietnam*: Can Tho, Cam Ranh, Dalat, Danang, Saigon. From *Singapore*: Singapore. From *Sri Lanka*: Panadura, Tala-

wakelie. From *Thailand*: Bangkok, Pitsanulok. From the *United States*: Anaheim, Anchorage, Bellevue, Burbank, Carson, Charlottesville (Indiana), Culver City, El Cajon, Fairbanks, Foster City, Fresno, Fullerton, Gardena, Hawaii County, Hawthorne, Hayward, Honolulu, Hood River, Kenai, La Mirada, Lomita, Long Beach, Los Angeles, Maui County, New York, Novato, Oakland, Pleasant Hill, Portland, Riverside, Sacramento, San Diego, San Francisco, San Pablo, Santa Fe Springs, Santa Rosa, Seattle, Seward, South San Francisco, Tacoma.

4. All but one corporation had its offices in Honolulu.

5. Basic information may be obtained in Pacific Islands Tourism Development Council, *Charter of Incorporation* (Honolulu: Department of Regulatory Agencies, State of Hawaii, August 11, 1976); Pacific Islands Tourism Development Council, *By-Laws of Pacific Islands Tourism Development Council* (Honolulu: Department of Regulatory Agencies, State of Hawaii, 1976); Pacific Islands Tourism Development Council, *Minutes of the Pacific Islands Tourism Development Council, Board of Directors Meeting* (Honolulu: Department of Planning and Economic Development, State of Hawaii, irregular, 1976–1979).

6. Basic information may be obtained in Pacific Islands Conference, *Proceedings of the Pacific Islands Conference: Development of the Pacific Way, March 26–28, 1980* (Honolulu: Pacific Islands Development Program, 1980); Pacific Islands Conference, *Proceedings of the Second Pacific Islands Conference: Development and Change* (Honolulu: Pacific Islands Development Program, 1985); Pacific Islands Conference, Standing Committee, *Report of the Pacific Islands Conference Standing Committee* (Honolulu: Pacific Islands Development Program, irregular, 1980–).

7. Uentabo F. Neemia, *Cooperation and Conflict: Costs, Benefits and National Interests in Pacific Regional Cooperation* (Suva: Institute for Pacific Studies, University of the South Pacific, 1986), pp. 42–45.

THE SOUTH PACIFIC
CANNOT LIVE WITHOUT THE
UNITED NATIONS BUT
SOMETIMES CANNOT LIVE
WITH IT: TWO REGIONAL
SPIN-OFFS

INTRODUCTION

The South Pacific Commission, as noted above, was a regional initiative that took place because the United Nations had not set up an economic commission for the South Pacific. When various UN Specialized Agencies began to establish offices on a regional basis, none of their regional headquarters was in the South Pacific. The Regional Office for the Western Pacific of the World Health Organization (WHO), for example, is at Manila. Some area offices, notably one for WHO, were located at Sydney to cover the South Pacific. It took some time before UN offices of any sort were situated on the soil of a Pacific island country. In view of the immense need for UN technical assistance in the region, two regional organizations in the South Pacific emerged. The South Pacific Labour Ministers' Conference (SPLMC) was established to provide better liaison with the International Labor Organization (ILO). The Committee for Co-ordination of Joint Prospecting for Mineral Resources in South Pacific Offshore Areas (CCOP/SOPAC) began as a subsidiary body of the UN Economic Commission for Asia and the Far East (ECAFE) at Bangkok, but in due course countries of the region found a juridically separate institution desirable. This chapter describes these two organizations.

SOUTH PACIFIC LABOUR MINISTERS' CONFERENCE[1]

In 1966 the Conference of Asian Labor Ministers (CALM) was established to advise the International Labor Organization (ILO) Regional Office at Bangkok on how to devote more resources to Asian countries. CALM succeeded to some extent in attracting more project assistance for Asia. With this example in mind, Australian Prime Minister Gough Whitlam, during a meeting of the South Pacific Forum in 1973, proposed a Conference of South Pacific Labour Ministers, as there was no ILO Area Office in the Pacific islands at the time. Later the same year, Sydney was the site for the first such meeting.

There is no formal constitution or terms of reference for SPLMC. The practice is for member countries to identify priorities so that ILO can provide more appropriate services for the region. Otherwise, the Ministers meet to exchange views on key problems of employment, industrial relations, and world economic conditions.

South Pacific Labour Ministers Conferences were held yearly from 1973 to 1976, then in 1978 and 1979; the 1978 Conference agreed that meetings would occur at biennial intervals after 1979. The host country provides a secretariat for the Conference. A Chairman and Vice Chairman are elected at each meeting, and members of a Drafting Committee are selected to prepare the Communiqué. The head of the delegation of the country hosting the conference chairs the meeting. The ILO Regional Office at Suva serves in a coordinating role in regard to specific projects but is not formally a part of SPLMC. In 1981 the Conference asked the South Pacific Forum to designate the South Pacific Bureau for Economic Co-operation (SPEC) as SPLMC's secretariat, but this suggestion was not accepted.

There is no formal membership procedure. Fifteen countries were at the inaugural meeting in 1973, but not all of these countries have attended in recent years (Table 10.1). Most countries are represented by ministers of labor, as they do not yet have fully active trade unions or employer organizations, which would be required to follow the ILO pattern of tripartite representation. Observers from various international organizations have attended on a regular basis, notably ILO, the South Pacific Commission (SPC), South Pacific Bureau for Economic Co-operation (SPEC), and the UN Development Program (UNDP).

In accordance with the Pacific Way, when Conferences are in Australia or New Zealand, costs of accommodation are paid by the host ministry of labor, which can afford to do so; at other sites, delegations pay their own expenses. Otherwise, there is no budget for the organization. Special projects have been financed by ILO, SPC, SPEC, or UNDP, according to their own priorities, outside the framework of the Conference.

The Conferences are primarily forums for dialog. The following topics have been discussed in recent years: employment potential of small-scale and rural enterprises, facilitating a smoother transition from

Table 10.1
South Pacific Labour Ministers Conference: Membership

Year Joined	Participating Countries	Inactive Since
1973	American Samoa	1978
	Australia	1978
	Cook Islands	
	Fiji	
	Guam	1974
	Kiribati (joined as Gilbert Islands)	
	Nauru	
	New Zealand	
	Papua New Guinea	
	Solomon Islands (joined as British Solomon Islands)	
	Tonga	
	Trust Territory of the Pacific Islands	1976
	Tuvalu (joined as Ellice Islands)	1981
	Vanuatu (joined as New Hebrides)	1981
	Western Samoa	
Totals	15-6=9 countries	

school to work, labor productivity, and urban drift. Other subjects of discussion have been reports prepared by other organizations, such as ILO and SPC. Participants define regional priorities and evaluate projects funded by ILO, SPEC, and UNDP at the formal sessions as well as through informal discussions.

Through the urging of SPLMC, ILO and SPC have jointly completed two projects. One is a report on mobility of labor in the South Pacific. The second project is a directory of training facilities for the region.

Although SPLMC is an outgrowth of CALM, and was proposed at a meeting of the South Pacific Forum, CALM was renamed the Conference of Asian and Pacific Labor Ministers (CAPLM) in 1966, three years after SPLMC began. Both CAPLM and SPLMC were organized at the encouragement of ILO; in the case of CAPLM, the Regional Office in Bangkok was a catalyst, whereas the Area Office that opened at Suva in 1975 came after the desire to form SPLMC. In 1978 ILO renamed its Bangkok office from Asian Regional Department to the Regional Department for Asia and the Pacific, reflecting the same trend. As there was no reason for two similar meetings each year, the two organizations held Conferences in alternate years between 1976 and 1984; SPLMC has not met since 1983. The Pacific Way permeates the discussions throughout.

COMMITTEE FOR CO-ORDINATION OF JOINT PROSPECTING FOR MINERAL RESOURCES IN SOUTH PACIFIC OFFSHORE AREAS[2]

Most Asian and Pacific countries have large seacoasts and thus have a potential for mineral deposits in the seabed adjacent to the coastline. Few Asian and Pacific countries have sufficient experts to prospect for petroleum and other minerals. In 1965, accordingly, the Committee on Mineral Resources of the UN Economic Commission for Asia and the Pacific (ECAFE) called together a meeting of experts to discuss how to coordinate surveys of offshore minerals so that the countries themselves would derive benefits rather than having to contract such work to foreign corporations on a piecemeal basis. The result was the establishment in mid-1966 of the Committee for Co-ordination of Joint Prospecting for Mineral Resources in Asian Offshore Areas (CCOP).

CCOP was established to coordinate the search for mineral deposits in the seabed of ECAFE member countries. In 1968 oil was discovered in Tonga. Discussion regarding a separate CCOP for the South Pacific was first mooted in August 1970, during a session of ECAFE's Working Party of Senior Geologists and the ECAFE Subcommittee on Mineral Resources Development at Bandung, when a delegate from Fiji noted that countries in the South Pacific had an urgent need to locate sources of foreign exchange yet had virtually unstudied seabeds stretching over a vast area of the Pacific Ocean. Fiji proposed that ECAFE set up a special South Pacific body similar to CCOP, and the idea was supported by Australia, New Zealand, and Papua New Guinea, then approved at the April 1971, Session of ECAFE. After a Preparatory Meeting at Manila during July 17–21, 1971, the Inaugural Session of CCOP/SO-PAC met at Suva between November 7 and 13, 1972, where Terms of Reference of the Committee for Co-ordination of Joint Prospecting for Mineral Resources in South Pacific Offshore Areas were approved.

CCOP/SOPAC originally operated in the manner of a subsidiary body of the UN's regional commission in Bangkok, known as the Economic and Social Commission for Asia and the Pacific (ESCAP) after 1974. Over the first decade, when priorities of the region did not always mesh comfortably with those of UN funding agencies, CCOP/SOPAC member countries began to think of the advantages of having the organization operate independently. For example, in 1981 the South Pacific Forum supported the Solomon Islands' objections to a geophysical and ocean-ographic survey by a vessel of the Soviet Union, as suggested by ES-CAP. Accordingly, CCOP/SOPAC members agreed to establish an autonomous body, while keeping the name of the organization intact; the decision was made during the twelfth CCOP/SOPAC Session at Nuku'alofa, Tonga, during October 11–20, 1983. Terms of Reference for the organization were revised, and a Memorandum of Understand-ing declaring CCOP/SOPAC to be outside the UN system was prepared for acceptance by member countries at a special session of the Com-mittee in Rarotonga during May 23–25, 1984. The new CCOP/SOPAC, thus, officially began work as a separate international organization at the Rarotonga meeting. The current Terms of Reference of CCOP/ SOPAC specify the functions of the organization to be as follows: "pro-mote, coordinate, plan and implement geological, geophysical, energy studies and other related natural resource prospecting projects and basic investigations in the onshore, coastal and adjoining offshore areas of the member countries as well as the oceanic areas of the region."

The highest organ is the Committee of National Representatives (Figure 10.1), whose Chairman is the prime mover of the organization throughout the year. Industry Ministers and other governmental rep-resentatives attend a ten-day Annual Session each year. The Annual Session begins with an open Plenary Session, and a closed Special Session of members meets next. As the UN Educational, Scientific, and Cultural Organization (UNESCO) sponsors the International Ocean-ographic Commission (IOC) to coordinate studies of the sort undertaken by CCOP/SOPAC, scientists at the General Session then convene in the Joint CCOP/SOPAC-IOC Working Group on South Pacific Tecton-ics and Resources (STAR) to review research findings and needs for

Figure 10.1
Organization of the Committee for Co-ordination of Joint Prospecting for Mineral Resources in South Pacific Offshore Areas

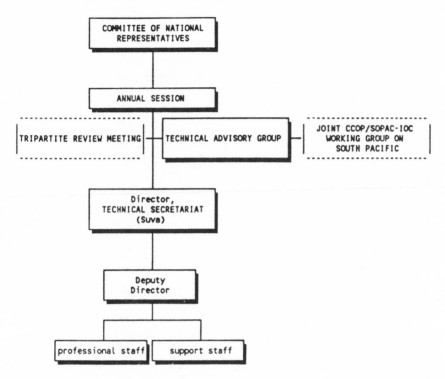

the region. The Technical Advisory Group (TAG) of government and donor agency technocrats then identifies projects suggested by STAR that are likely to promote development in the region, proposing a CCOP/SOPAC Work List for approval by the Committee in its final Plenary Session. During the Annual Session, the Tripartite Review Meeting (TRM) of governments and funding agencies review progress in the UN-funded research. At the Annual Session, each member designates a national representative to serve on the Committee in order to maintain liaison with the Technical Secretariat during the following year.

A Technical Secretariat (Techsec) for CCOP/SOPAC has been in Suva since 1974. A Director and Deputy Director head Techsec, which employs 13 professional and 16 support staff.

Originally, membership was open to ESCAP members in the South Pacific. At the inaugural meeting of CCOP/SOPAC in 1972, six countries attended as members (Table 10.2); technical advisers from Australia, France, the United Kingdom, and the United States were also

Table 10.2
Committee for Co-ordination of Joint Prospecting for Mineral Resources in South Pacific
Offshore Areas: Membership and Finances

Year Joined	Member Countries	Contributions (1988)
1972	Fiji	9.1%
	New Zealand	9.1
	Papua New Guinea	9.1
	Solomon Islands (joined as British Solomon Islands)	9.1
	Tonga	9.1
	Western Samoa	9.1
1973	Cook Islands	9.1
1975	Kiribati (joined as Gilbert Islands)	2.3
1978	Vanuatu (joined as New Hebrides)	9.1
1981	Guam^a	9.1
1983	Tuvalu	6.8
1986	Australia	12.8
Totals	12 Members	$80,385

^aobserver in 1980.

present. Indonesia, Japan, New Hebrides (now Vanuatu), and the Philippines sent observers to the Preparatory Meeting but did not join at that time. In later years, five countries joined while the organization still operated as a UN body. Nauru and successor states of the Trust Territory of the Pacific Islands have been Observers since 1978. After CCOP/SOPAC became independent of the United Nations, Australia joined as a full member in 1986. Technical advisers have come from Australia, Canada, China, France, Japan, New Zealand, Norway, the Soviet Union, the United Kingdom, the United States, and West Germany as well as from ESCAP, IOC, UNDP, SPEC, the South Pacific Forum Fisheries Agency (SPFFA), and the University of the South Pacific (USP).

Each country has contributed about the same amount for the administrative budget of Techsec since the organization became autonomous (Table 10.2). UNDP has been the principal source of project funds for CCOP/SOPAC. The allotment for 1979–81 was $2.5 million, for 1982–86 was $3 million, and is currently somewhat below previous levels. The UNDP Project Manager headed Techsec when it was a UN project; currently he is Deputy Director. The European Economic Community (EEC) has provided 5 million European Currency Units (about US$4 million) for the 1986–90 period; Canada has donated C$10 million (US $ 8 million) for 1988–93; and the United States approved $200,000 for 1987–90. In all, international agencies contribute about $1 million annually. In addition, in-kind project support has been provided by the Commonwealth Fund for Technical Co-operation (CFTC).

Initially, CCOP/SOPAC sought mineral deposits in the seabed in offshore areas of South Pacific countries, chartering oceanographic vessels to engage in offshore resource mapping in 1976–81 for cobalt, manganese, and phosphate deposits; this work is now carried on by a Tripartite Programme of Australia, New Zealand, and the United States, which has prospected for oil; Japan now assists this effort. In 1980 CCOP/SOPAC began onshore prospecting for clay. Recent mineral prospecting has searched for hydrocarbons, precious corals, and minerals with more immediate commercial potential, though the cost of extraction is still high. In addition to seabed mapping, CCOP/SOPAC pursues projects related to coastal development, collecting data on engineering baselines, geological hazards and erosion, and wavepower. Techsec analyzes data collected by its professional staff with assistance from scientists from member and nonmember countries.

Annual Sessions prepare the Work List of tasks for each year. There has been progress in locating cobalt, manganese, metalliferous sediment, petroleum, phosphate, phosphorus, polymetallic sulphides, and precious corals thus far. Reports have also been prepared on alternative energy resources, coastal development and management, deep-sea drilling, geological hazards, law of the sea, marine pollution, mineral resources, remote sensing, and seismicity.

Since its inception CCOP/SOPAC has provided training programs and workshops to develop more technical expertise in the region; 38 man-years of training were completed by the end of 1986. In recent years Annual Workshops have occurred at the time of the Annual Session. In 1987 a Fellowship Scheme began, offering short-term assignments at Techsec to persons from island member countries. Some training courses are at Suva, some aboard ship, and some at institutions and training centers abroad. The organization offers a Certificate in Earth Science and Marine Geology.

Over time Techsec and delegates attending CCOP/SOPAC Sessions agreed that the goals of the organization required funding beyond that provided by UN agencies. ESCAP's bureaucratistic modus operandi was antithetical to the Pacific Way that gradually permeated the organization, which broke free as a result. In 1988 the Forum asked CCOP/SOPAC to sit on the new South Pacific Organisations Co-ordinating Committee (SPOCC), thereby making CCOP/SOPAC subsidiary to the Forum. Although CCOP/SOPAC is a coordinator of studies, as its name implies, it primarily initiates new work; at the same time, it works in close collaboration with related projects. In due course there will be much of value to interest the private sector in undertaking follow-up work to exploit the mineral resources.

CONCLUSION

Both SPLMC and CCOP/SOPAC now exist apart from the formal structure of the United Nations. ILO itself urged the formation of the Asian Labor Ministers Conference and was delighted when SPLMC arose as well. CCOP/SOPAC severed ties with ESCAP on good terms, but there was more of a divorce than a simple devolution of authority, as the various layers of bureaucracy in the United Nations for approving new studies had become a source of considerable frustration to Techsec. Financial support from UN agencies continues for projects in both cases, but CCOP/SOPAC is able to attract other funding without having to tug at its former umbilical cord. A Pacific Way solution was found for both organizations.

NOTES

1. Basic information may be obtained in South Pacific Labour Ministers' Conference, *Report of the South Pacific Labour Ministers' Conference* (1973, 1974, 1976, 1978, 1979, 1981, 1983).

2. Basic information may be obtained in Committee for Co-ordination of Joint Prospecting of Mineral Resources in South Pacific Offshore Areas, *A Memorandum to Confer Upon the Committee for Co-ordination of Investigations of Mineral Resources in South Pacific Offshore Areas Status as an Intergovernmental Organization* (Rarotonga, May 23–25, 1984); Committee for Co-ordination of Joint Prospecting of Mineral Resources in South Pacific Offshore Areas, *Terms of Reference of the Committee for Co-ordination of Joint Prospecting of Mineral Resources in South Pacific Offshore Areas* (Rarotonga, May 23–25, 1984); Committee for Co-ordination of Joint Prospecting of Mineral Resources in South Pacific Offshore Areas, *Proceedings of the Session* (Bangkok: Economic and Social Commission for Asia and the Pacific, annually, 1972–1984; issued by the Technical Secretariat in Suva since 1985); Committee for Co-ordination of Joint Prospecting of Mineral Resources in South Pacific Offshore Areas, *Summary of CCOP/SOPAC Activities, 1975–1985* (Suva: Technical Secretariat, 1985).

11 NEWEST KID ON THE BLOCK: TOURISM COUNCIL OF THE SOUTH PACIFIC

ORIGINS[1]

Tourism, a source of foreign exchange for many South Pacific island nations, was a topic on the agenda of the initial meeting of the South Pacific Forum in 1971. In 1972 the Forum discussed the adverse effects of tourism on the way of life of the island peoples of the region and supported a proposal at the South Pacific Conference for a UN study on the subject. Thereafter, the Forum allowed tourism development to be pursued nationally. However, attracting travelers from distant locations, such as Japan and the United States, is an objective far beyond the means of any single country in the region. The resulting study commissioned by the UN Development Program (UNDP) proposed tourist associations for Melanesia, Micronesia, and Polynesia as well as for the South Pacific region as a whole, but this proposal was not pursued.

The South Pacific Bureau for Economic Co-operation (SPEC) prepared a preliminary project outline on tourist promotion in 1975 and a regional tourism brochure in 1977, when a Working Party on Tourism began work to explore regional efforts. Although SPEC commissioned a South Pacific Tourism Study, which reported in 1978, no definite proposals for an intergovernmental tourism organization were accepted by the end of 1978, and the Working Party was dissolved.

Meanwhile, the Melanesian Tourist Federation, Pacific Islands Tourism Development Council (discussed in Chapter 9), Micronesia Regional Tourism Council, and the Marketing Authority of Polynesia formed and dissolved. In 1982, when the European Economic Com-

Figure 11.1
Organization of the Tourism Council for the South Pacific

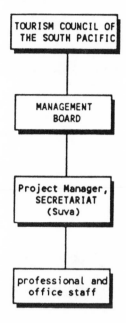

munity (EEC) showed interest in supporting projects in tourism development, the Pacific Asia Travel Association (PATA)—based at San Francisco between 1951 and 1986—arranged to cosponsor a Regional Tourism Meeting with SPEC at Suva from May 24–26, 1982, to identify areas of need. Malakai Gucake of the Fiji Visitor's Bureau (FVB) then took the leadership in proposing a draft of the Agreement Establishing the Tourism Council of the South Pacific (TCSP), which was signed at the founding session of the Council at Suva on March 21, 1983.

STRUCTURE

The preamble to the founding Agreement charges TCSP with the goal to "develop through cooperation, the tourism industries of the South Pacific and by doing so, seek to foster travel in the region." The plenary organ is the Council (Figure 11.1), which holds an annual meeting and elects a Chairman.

The principal office is the Secretariat, which is at Suva. Originally, it was in the FVB office, since TCSP's President was Malakai Gucake, then head of FVB. With the success of TCSP in attracting EEC funds for the Pacific Regional Tourism Development Programme (PRTDP), the Chair rotated to Tonga in 1985, and in 1986 the Secretariat was located in a building on the grounds of SPEC, where the EEC Project

Table 11.1
Tourism Council of the South Pacific: Membership and Finances

Year Joined	Member Countries	Contributions (1988)
1983	American Samoa	8.6%
	Cook Islands	13.9
	Fiji	17.1
	Niue	1.2
	Tahiti	13.9[a]
	Tonga	5.7
	Western Samoa	8.6
1984	Papua New Guinea	11.8
	Solomon Islands	5.7
	Vanuatu	11.3
1986	Kiribati	1.2
	Tuvalu	1.2
Totals	12 Members	$91,538

Manager is in charge of the staff. In 1985 the Council anticipated the need to monitor the EEC project, so it established a Management Board in Suva to maintain contact with the Secretariat on behalf of the Council.

MEMBERSHIP AND FINANCES

According to the Agreement establishing TCSP, there were seven founding members (Table 11.1). Later in 1984 three additional countries signed the Agreement, and two more joined when PRTDP began. There is a provision for Associate Members, which can include corporations and nonprofit organizations identified with the international visitor industry. So far no Associate Members have joined.

Assessments of members for regional counterpart staff (Table 11.1) are based on their "proportionate share in the overall operation of the Council" [Article VII(2)]; in 1988 this amounted to F$119,000 (US$91,538), but most funds have come from outside sources. SPEC officially applied for EEC funding on behalf of TCSP. EEC will provide a total of about somewhat more than one million European Currency Units (US$1.2 million) each year until 1991, though American Samoa, the Cook Islands, and Niue participate in PRTDP through Australian and New Zealand assistance. Tahiti has not yet contributed sufficient amounts to be included in the full scope of the project.

PROJECTS

The main TCSP project, the Pacific Regional Tourism Development Programme, is funded by EEC. A major focus is institution building—to establish a tourism research, information, and training infrastructure so that the industry can operate on its own after external funding ends. A data base of tourism facilities and tourist traffic is computerized, and data collection is now standardized for entry into the central data base at the Secretariat. Surveys of visitors are being conducted. The Secretariat has developed packets of materials to familiarize the trainers of tourism employees with operational aspects of tourism, such as catering and tour operators. Curriculum materials are available for use in the social studies courses in the region. Documentary films and slides have been produced for marketing and promotional purposes. The project provides technical assistance to national visitor's bureaus in each TCSP member country.

IMPLICATIONS

After the efforts of the South Pacific Forum and SPEC, including the joint PATA/SPEC meeting in 1982, TCSP in effect superseded the former PITDC. TCSP was necessary as a separate organization to highlight the fervent desire for something to be done, and progress is occurring. Coordination of various efforts is in accordance with the Pacific Way principle that South Pacific solutions are to be found for South Pacific needs.

However, in certain quarters the view is expressed that there is too much overlap if not duplication of effort throughout the organizations of the South Pacific region. The Pacific Islands Conference (PIC) has authorized a study of long-range projections on tourism for the region and to inventory existing facilities combined with some training of tourist management personnel; these activities appear to duplicate the activities of TCSP. PIC's overlap with TCSP is not a particularly glaring example, but it is perhaps a useful one. We turn in the final chapter to an analysis of the proposal for a single regional organization in the South Pacific into which all the various bodies might be included together.

NOTE

1. Basic information can be obtained in Tourism Council of the South Pacific, *Minutes, Meeting of the Tourism Council of the South Pacific* (annually, 1983–).

12   *THE FUTURE OF SOUTH PACIFIC REGIONAL COOPERATION*

CONFLICTING FORCES IN THE REGION

The road between the South Pacific Health Service and the Tourism Council for the South Pacific has taken some 40 years to travel. Technical organizations predominate, and indeed their viability encouraged the formation of the South Pacific Forum as a multipurpose regional effort with explicitly political objectives. Yet the many activities of the South Pacific Commission and the proliferation of various regional organizations also outside the framework of the Forum have presented some difficulties.

First, South Pacific countries with populations of 15,000 or so have limited budgets and cannot afford to send their top officials on airplane trips to meetings at several times in the year to suit the convenience of a variety of institutions. Second, there is inevitable overlap between the regional organizations, and a clear delineation of respective areas of activity is not always possible; several bodies, for example, have discussed proposals for a single judicial appeals system for the South Pacific. Third, Noumea is an unpopular site for the headquarters of the South Pacific Commission: countries of the South Pacific would prefer to boycott French territories until Paris stops testing nuclear weapons in the region and gives a larger measure of local autonomy to French Polynesia, New Caledonia, and Wallis and Futuna, the major remaining remnants of empire among the Pacific islands. Fourth, there are so many agencies involved in regional institutions, from education ministries to police departments, that ministries of foreign affairs often do not know what is going on. Fifth, external sources can determine priorities of projects for the region by selecting an appropriate autonomous body to support rather than providing institutional support to a single regional organization. Sixth, officials in charge of organizations that lack a secretariat often place their international responsibilities on a back burner while dealing with more pressing immediate domestic problems, then go to regional meeting without being adequately prepared to commit their countries.

A SINGLE REGIONAL ORGANIZATION?

The various difficulties are overdramatized in my opinion, as there are benefits to overlapping organizations.[1] If modest budgets limit air travel, first of all, this can be a source of pressure so that meetings will be truly useful lest attendance will be low. Second, several bodies can examine the same functional area from different angles; if two institutions agree on the need for a project, it will be more worthy of support than if only one organization does so. Therefore, a sort of institutional system of checks and balances will exist to keep each organization on its toes. Third, as long as Noumea is the headquarters of SPC, countries of the South Pacific will derive funds from France and can exert continuing pressure on Paris to end nuclear weapons tests in the region and to grant independence to French territories in the region. Fourth, ministries of foreign affairs should not monopolize regional cooperation; other ministries should have an opportunity as well. Fifth, external sources can determine priorities of projects for the region whether there are many or few regional organizations. Sixth, a secretariat can often overcentralize power in a regional organization; the tension between institutional bureaucrats and ministerial decision makers will ultimately be resolved by the latter.

The idea of a clear and neat organizational structure for South Pacific regional cooperation may seem desirable on paper. However, the reasons for the topsy-like growth of regional institutions are often overlooked. No region in the world has a rationalized structure for institutional cooperation, and the amount of duplication within the supposedly more unified UN system is well known by knowledgeable observers. The real reason for talk of a single regional organization is the desire to reassign functions of the South Pacific Commission to institutions more in keeping with the Pacific Way. In 1987 the South Pacific Forum decided to set up a new Committee on Regional Institutional Arrangements (CRIA)—composed of SPC, SPEC, USP, and possibly other institutions—with a view to designing a more rational structure that would enable the various functions of SPC to be transferred elsewhere in due course. In 1988 the Forum established the South Pacific Organisations Co-ordinating Committee (SPOCC) to include CCOP/SOPAC, SPC, SPFFA, and USP; SPC put off action on the proposal to 1989, but the remaining organizations in effect became subsidiary to the Forum, whose Secretariat chairs SPOCC. Thus, a more useful agenda is a discussion on the extent to which new regional organizations are needed, a subject to which we now turn.

THE UNFINISHED BUSINESS OF SOUTH PACIFIC REGIONAL COOPERATION

The future of regional cooperation in the South Pacific will be more constructively advanced by noting the many needed gaps in the scope of regional activities rather than by tidying up supposed overlapping jurisdictions. While experts on regional cooperation differ in specifying lists of possible issue areas for international cooperation, one can derive a clue on the future of South Pacific international development by looking for parallels with the history of regional cooperation in nearby Asia.[2]

The Colombo Plan, for example, started with an objective similar to SPEC; lacking a superordinate body similar to the South Pacific Forum, the Colombo Plan remained largely a paper organization until it established an institute to train educators at technical training institutes for its member countries, a function performed by the University of the South Pacific. The decline of the South-East Asian Treaty Organization (SEATO) appears to parallel that of ANZUS. The Association of South East Asian Nations (ASEAN) and the South Asian Association for Regional Cooperation (SAARC) might be compared with the South Pacific Forum and SPEC, though ASEAN and SAARC have much to learn from the highly pragmatic, result-oriented modus operandi of SPEC. ASEAN's search for regional industries in the 1980s was unspectacular until the organization decided to provide tax and trade preference advantages for joint ventures among countries of the region with a large percentage of outside investment capital. SAARC has sought to provide regional training opportunities in various technical fields at national institutions that formerly were closed to students and technocrats from bordering countries.

Some of the less well-known Asian regional organizations, however, provide better models for the South Pacific to consider. One major gap in the South Pacific appears to be in the field of food production. The Afro-Asian Rural Reconstruction Organization (AARRO) seeks to assist farmers in forming cooperatives and otherwise becoming economically self-sufficient and politically powerful, the Centre on Integrated Rural Development for Asia and the Pacific (CIRDAP) encourages macro-level planning in agriculture for large countries, the Food and Fertilizer Technology Center for the Asian and Pacific Region (FFTC) is a kind of international extension service for farmers. The Southeast Asian Fisheries Development Center (SEAFDEC), meanwhile, provides training on techniques of aquaculture as well as deep-sea fishing and post-harvest technology; these tasks might be a logical extension of the activities of the South Pacific Forum Fisheries Agency (SPFFA).

A second obvious need is educational—to generate effective curricula and teaching materials in the fields of fine arts, languages, medicine, mathematics and science—the objective of regional centers under the framework of the Southeast Asian Ministers of Education Organization (SEAMEO). The South Pacific Board for Educational Assessment (SPBEA) appears to be heading in this direction. Related functions are performed in fine arts by the Cultural and Social Center for the Asian and Pacific Region (CULSOCEN), which has expressed an interest in attracting new members from the South Pacific. The central banks of the South Pacific might find joint meetings, such as those of the Southeast Asian Central Banks Group (SEACEN), to be useful opportunities to plan together or vehicles for attracting funds to establish a regional center to train bureaucrats in matters of finance and banking. Papua New Guinea already belongs to SEACEN's close cousin, the Central Banks of Southeast Asia, Australia, and New Zealand (SEANZA).

South Pacific countries already belong to several Asian regional organizations, bearing witness to needs of the South Pacific that are unfilled within the region. SPLMC began after the Conference of Asian Labor Ministers (CALM) had been in existence for over a decade. The Asian-Pacific Parliamentarians' Union (APPU) added nearly ten South Pacific members in the last decade, mostly those from the Association of Pacific Island Legislatures (APIL). The Asian-African Legal Consultative Committee (AALCC) provides a forum to discuss legal issues before the International Law Commission and UN bodies; AALCC, in consultation with South Pacific countries, virtually wrote the Law of the Sea Treaty. The Asian Productivity Organization (APO), which provides short-term training in methods of increased productivity in agriculture and manufacturing for small- and medium-scale enterprises, has Fiji as a member. The Asian-Pacific Postal Union (APPU), with Papua New Guinea as a member, assists countries in improving postal services, and a restricted postal union for the South Pacific would doubtless be welcomed by the Universal Postal Union (UPU).

In some cases, the resources of the South Pacific are not at a level where separate institutions are immediately anticipated. The Asian Development Bank (ADB) is one such organization; more than ten South Pacific countries are now members, and ADB established a regional office at Port Vila, Vanuatu, in 1985. The Asian Reinsurance Corporation (AsianRe) underwrites insurance companies within the region without draining away foreign exchange, but the volume of insurance needs within the South Pacific has not yet reached a critical level. The Association for Science Cooperation in Asia (ASCA) brings together scientists from government laboratories—perhaps a luxury in the South Pacific today. At the same time, the need to cope with pests in agriculture and forestry, as well as pollution in fishing, suggests that the South Pacific might consolidate some of SPC's scientific projects into a new institution. If several governments fear a population explosion in the South Pacific, the defunct Regional Organization for Inter-governmental Co-operation and Co-ordination in Family and Population Planning in Southeast Asia (IGCC) provides a useful model. If massive tax cheating becomes a problem in the South Pacific, the Study Group on Asian Tax Administration and Research (SGATAR) or the Taxation and Customs Cooperation Conference (TCCC) might appear relevant to the region.

Yet another category of regional institution is the commodity community. Asian organizations exist to promote the fortunes of coconuts, jute, natural rubber, pepper, tin, and vegetables. The Pacific Islands Producers' Association (PIPA) began as a banana cartel. Several South Pacific countries belong to the Asian and Pacific Coconut Community (APCC), but the other resources are unavailable in any significant quantity in the region today, though CCOP/SOPAC may locate some new minerals in the seas near island nations of the region. Finally, no interest has been expressed in a SEATO for the South Pacific now that ANZUS has evaporated.

The Melanesian Spearhead Group and the proposed Polynesian Economic and Cultural Community are part of an unfinished agenda as well, but may have a useful role to play. Within Asia, the six-nation ASEAN was preceded by the successful Association of Southeast Asia (ASA), composed of Malaya, Philippines, and Thailand; ASEAN copied the organizational structure and spirit of cooperation that began in ASA. Unlike Africa, the Arab world, and Latin America, Asia has not developed a pan-regional political institution; in due course an ASEAN-SAARC merger may take place, but only after careful preparation. Africa and Latin America have found their regional political organizations to be too large to forge a happy consensus on a wide variety of issues, while the Arab world and the South Pacific have had more solidarity. Yet in all cases the political institutions are paralleled by surrounding technical organizations, where contentious issues are seldom raised. If the South Pacific backtracks to subregionalism, there is precedent in the experience of regional cooperation; a negotiated compromise between subregions may carry more weight than a weak consensus among all countries.

As most South Pacific regional organizations have headquarters in Fiji, one effect of subregionalization could be a dispersion in the locus of organizational efforts to other countries. Fiji plans to join neither the Melanesian nor the Polynesian groupings, holding out for the primacy of the South Pacific Forum and similar pan-regional bodies. However, the 1987 coup in Fiji has changed the situation somewhat. The leadership of Fiji in the region has been questioned, as other countries are not eager to experience a coup based on extraconstitutional processes. The devaluation of the Fiji dollar caused retrenchment in budgets of organizations that collected assessments in Fiji dollars, though of course another currency could be selected with ease. However, some institutions may find that it is more cost-effective to relocate to other countries. In addition, the departure of many well-educated expatriates and Indians from Fiji means that clerical and professional personnel may be less available to staff regional organizations, though so far only USP has suffered a visible loss in this regard. Fiji's claim to the lion's share of "South Pacificrats" has been merely one of convenience thus far. One theory of regional cooperation stresses that a country playing a leadership role must make economic sacrifices lest its centrality becomes an issue in due course.[3] Thus, one of the unfinished tasks of South Pacific regional cooperation will be to manage these tensions.

THE PACIFIC WAY AS A NEW THEORY OF INTERNATIONAL INTEGRATION

If the South Pacific is destined to have more rather than fewer regional organizations, the primary reason is that a new form of international statecraft has developed in the region. This innovation, known as the Pacific Way, goes beyond previous theories of international integration.

Unlike other regions of the world, the South Pacific would suffer greatly if regional cooperation were to disappear; the South Pacific Forum and other bodies are not luxuries but instead are imperatives for countries with small populations almost totally lacking in lucrative cash crops. Pooling resources to rationalize external assistance has an appealing logic, but there is a cultural basis for cooperation in the region that transcends pragmatic considerations.

Theories of political integration speculate on factors accounting for the development of peaceful linkages between countries and peoples.[4] Although interest in peaceful linkages can be traced to the various plans for peace of Dante Alighieri, the duc de Sully, Immanuel Kant, and others, modern social science theorizing about political integration dates from 1946, when British Prime Minister Winston Churchill delivered a speech in Zurich, urging the development of "some kind of United States of Europe." The follow-up to Churchill's address was an increase in enthusiasm for the idea of European integration as a pathway to peace, and academic researchers began to construct theories that might advance the goal of European political unification, with European economic integration as a preliminary step.

Theories of integration may be classified with reference to stages in the process of achieving greater harmony between peoples and states. Some scholars focus on *preconditions*, that is, on elements required before integration can move from stage I to stage II, from stage II to III, and so forth. A second focus is on *transaction flows*, that is, the rise and fall of trends in integrative behavior over time or over space; the latter concern consists of an identification of subclusters of countries with dense patterns of interaction. A third focus is on the *development of integrative processes* because of, or in spite of, the volume and percentages of international interactions or the presence of so-called preconditions. The third mode of analysis asks whether comembership in alliances leads to increased integration or decreased integration—and why.

Some of the initial criticisms of integration theory focused on its Eurocentrism, that is, its relevance to Europe and irrelevance elsewhere. Various preconditions to the formation of political or economic integration tended to set forth by such scholars as Karl Deutsch and Ernst Haas, and developed countries were predicted to be more likely to succeed in achieving integration.[5] Amitai Etzioni, on the other hand, felt that developing countries might be more successful at political integration because they have fewer vested interests in a nonprosperous status quo.[6] Roger Hansen, while agreeing with Etzioni, noted three specific problems.[7] First, economic issues are already heavily politicized in the Third World, so it is absurd to predict that an economic union can lead to a political union through gradual politicization, or so Hansen argued; instead, developing countries must depoliticize economic issues as a precondition to the success of economic unions. Second, the superpowers hamper the freedom of Third World countries to act by penetrating their economic and political systems. Third, integrative efforts will not be possible as long as developing countries are still engaged in nation building.

Additional research on Latin American efforts at integration by Ernst Haas and a coauthor tends to support the compatibility of conclusions regarding Europe and Latin America.[8] Michael Haas and James Schubert, meanwhile, find that the technoeconomic functionalism of David Mitrany as a first step toward more ambitious efforts describes the integrative progress in Asia, where unobtrusive, functionally specific, intergovernmental organizations have been more successful than politicized forums.[9]

The style of negotiation known as the Pacific Way has supplied an important element in functional theory by showing that the most promising form of discussion between countries seeking to improve relations begins with areas of agreement and moves to areas of ambiguity, but scrupulously avoids unfruitful areas for cooperation.

A moment's reflection will suffice to demonstrate the new relevance of integration theory for contemporary Third World efforts. Hansen's three points no longer apply. First, economic union is not the objective of groups of Third World states; instead, the age of the New International Economic Order (NIEO) has dawned, and Third World countries seek to advance their own economic self-interest vis-à-vis the First World by joint cooperative efforts, such as those exemplified by the increased prices declared by the Organization of Petroleum Exporting Countries (OPEC) in the 1970s. Second, the dependent status of the Third World prompts attention to the collective need for a less dependent status. Third, the era of exclusivist nationalism is largely over; no Third World country is strong enough to bring about prosperity on its own, so economic cooperation among developing countries (known as ECDC) is the most prominent element of NIEO today, as the First and Second Worlds have failed thus far to give any realistic support to the aims or projects of NIEO.

Summarizing at this point, we note that greater levels of political integration may be arrayed on a continuum that extends from increased contact between adjacent states (low-level integration) to political unification (high-level integration), with many intermediate levels. While Deutsch's students have tended to focus on such low-level phenomena as trade, tourist traffic, news media attention, and the like, other scholars have looked upon intergovernmental organizations as facilitators or arenas for joint action. The findings have been limited to analyses based on a few cases, so there is no definitive set of propositions in the literature thus far.

The principal theories of functional cooperation place differing emphases on communication patterns, cultural factors, political solidarity, and technoeconomic cooperation. Deutsch's theory stresses communication patterns as predictors of international cooperation in technical then political matters because nations that communicate together form a common culture. Ernst Haas' functionalism argues that as soon as political elites pragmatically agree on joint efforts to achieve economic rewards, technical cooperation will be possible, and intercountry communication will increase; cultural similarities are assumed and cannot be developed. The Pacific Way argues that cultural solidarity must be present before elites can build community among a region of states; when cultural affinities are first recognized as a modus operandi, leaders of states can develop common political resolve, at which point plans for economic and technical cooperation will be possible. Both Deutsch and Ernst Haas were attempting to account for the possible rise of a united Europe through the European Common Market, but no such unity developed, profit was the dominant motive of interstate cooperation as the European Economic Community evolved into the broader European Community and its various institutions.

A recurring criticism of South Pacific regional cooperation is that the lion's share of benefits have gone to the most developed states of the region.[10] Fiji as the host for most headquarter sites has been vulnerable to this criticism. There are several responses possible. One is that the criticism has not been based on calculations on a per capita basis: we expect countries with larger populations to derive more benefits. A second reality is that regional cooperation requires extensive travel, and the structure of airfare has favored centrally-located Fiji, though this may change in due course. A third point is that headquarters facilities are generally placed in countries that donate buildings and land, and that offer diplomatic privileges to expatriate staff; few countries in the region have been as generous as Fiji in this regard. However, the criticism is useful, an illustration of the Pacific Way principle of frankness leading to unanimous compromises; regional institutions, as a result, are acutely conscious of the need to prove that they provide benefits to all members.

The Pacific Way, therefore, offers an explanation for the success of South Pacific regional cooperation in the continuing survival and growth of intergovernmental institutions. The solidarity of the region has forced outside countries to take notice, and many regional institutions exist because funding sources in metropolitan countries now accept the priorities of South Pacific countries. According to this analysis, the future of institution building among the states in the South Pacific, perilous as it was in the beginning, appears very bright today. Those who point out conflicts and inequities in the politics of regional cooperation perform a valuable service in keeping dialog open for new options. It is the culture of South Pacific regional cooperation that provides the necessary resilience for small but justifiably proud nations in the middle of the Pacific to thrive in an otherwise difficult world.

NOTES

1. I am indebted to Martin Landau for this point, from a lecture presented to the UN University, Tokyo, June, 1978.

2. See Michael Haas, *The Asian Way to Peace: A Story of Regional Cooperation* (New York: Praeger, 1989).

3. Amitai Etzioni, *Political Unification* (New York: Holt, Rinehart, Winston, 1965); Mancur Olson, Jr., *The Logic of Collective Action: Public Goods and the Theory of Groups* (New York: Schocken, 1965).

4. See Michael Haas, "International Integration," *International Systems* (New York: Intext, 1974), Ch. 8.

5. Karl W. Deutsch, *Political Community at the International Level* (Garden City, N.Y.: Doubleday, 1954); Ernst B. Haas, *The Uniting of Europe* (Stanford, Calif.: Stanford University Press, 1958).

6. Etzioni, *Political Unification.*

7. Roger Hansen, "Regional Integration: Reflections on a Decade of Theoretical Efforts," *World Politics* XXXI (January, 1969): 242–71.

8. Ernst B. Haas and Philippe C. Schmitter, "Economics and Differential Patterns of Political Integration: Projections About Unity in Latin America," *International Political Communities.* ed. Amitai Etzioni (Garden City, N.Y.: Doubleday, 1966), pp. 259–99.

9. Michael Haas, "Dimensions of International Cooperation in Asia," *Basic Data of Asian Regional Organizations*, ed. Michael Haas (Dobbs Ferry, N.Y.: Oceana, 1985), Ch. 10; James Schubert, "Toward a 'Working Peace System' in Asia: Organizational Growth and State Participation in Asian Regionalism," *International Organization* XXXII (Spring, 1978): 425–62; David Mitrany, *A Working Peace System* (Chicago: Quadrangle, 1966).

10. Uentabo F. Neemia, *Cooperation and Conflict: Costs, Benefits and National Interests in Pacific Regional Cooperation* (Suva: Institute of Pacific Studies, University of the South Pacific, 1986), Ch. 5.

BIBLIOGRAPHY

Anon. *Ancient Hawaiian Civilization*. Tokyo: Tuttle, 1965.

Anon. "Solomons Vetoes Fiji," *Pacific Islands Monthly* LIX (February, 1988): 29.

Anon. "Why We're Uniting: The Melanesian Bloc View," *Islands Business* (Suva) XIV (April, 1988): 26–29.

Australia, Department of Foreign Affairs. *Treaty Series*. Canberra: Australian Government Publishing Service.

Australia, Victoria, Commissioner of Police. *Proceedings of the Conference of Commissioners of Police of Australasia and the South West Pacific Region*. Melbourne: Commissioner of Police, Victoria, Australia, 1903, 1921–1929, 1937, 1939–1941, annually from 1944.

Ball, Desmond. *A Suitable Piece of Real Estate: American Installations in Australia*. Sydney: Hale & Iremonger, 1980.

Chowning, Anne. *An Introduction to the Peoples and Cultures of Melanesia*. Menlo Park, Calif.: Cummings, 1977.

Committee for Co-ordination of Joint Prospecting of Mineral Resources in South Pacific Offshore Areas. *A Memorandum to Confer Upon the Committee for Co-ordination of Joint Prospecting for Mineral Resources in South Pacific Offshore Areas Status as an Intergovernmental Organization*. Raratonga: CCOP/SOPAC, May 23–25, 1984.

———. *Terms of Reference of the Committee for Co-ordination of Joint Prospecting for Mineral Resources in South Pacific Offshore Areas*. Rarotonga: CCOP/SOPAC, May 23–25, 1984.

———. *Proceedings of the Session*. Bangkok: Economic and Social Commission for Asia and the Pacific, annually, 1972–1984; Suva: Technical Secretariat, annually, 1985-.

———. *Summary of CCOP/SOPAC Activities. 1975–1985*. Suva: Technical Secretariat, 1985.

Conference of the South Pacific Chiefs of Police. *Minutes of the Conference of South Pacific Chiefs of Police.* Annually, 1970–.

Cook Islands/Niue/New Zealand Joint Shipping Service. *Agreed Report of Cook Islands/Niue/New Zealand Joint Shipping Service.* Annually, 1975–.

Coser, Louis. *The Functions of Social Conflict.* New York: Free Press, 1956.

Crocombe, Ronald G. *The Pacific Way.* Suva: Lotu Pasifika Productions, 1976.

Daws, Gavan. *Shoal of Time.* New York: Macmillan, 1968.

Deutsch, Karl W. *Political Community at the International Level.* Garden City, N.Y.: Doubleday, 1954.

Dibb, Paul. *Review of Australia's Defence Capabilities: Report to the Minister for Defence.* Canberra: Australian Government Publishing Service, March, 1986.

Elder, H. P. *Pacific Islands Producers' Association.* Suva: Pacific Islands Producers' Secretariat, March, 1971.

Etzioni, Amitai (ed.), *International Political Communities.* Garden City, N.Y.: Doubleday, 1966.

Etzioni, Amitai. *Political Unification.* New York: Holt, Rinehart, Winston, 1965.

Fry, Gregory E. "Regionalism and the International Politics of the South Pacific," *Pacific Affairs* LIX (Fall, 1980): 455–84.

Haas, Ernst B. *The Uniting of Europe.* Stanford, Calif. CA: Stanford University Press, 1958.

Haas, Michael. *The Asian Way to Peace: A Story of Regional Cooperation.* New York: Praeger, 1989.

———. *Basic Data of Asian Regional Organizations.* Dobbs Ferry, NY: Oceana, 1985.

———. *International Systems.* New Y(:, 1974.

Haas, Michael, and Kanahele, George   ~ts for Pacific Community," *Pacific Community* (Tokyo) VI (C   ): 83–93.

Hansen, Roger. "Regional Integration: a Decade of Theoretical Efforts," *World Politics* XXXI (January), 196:. 242–71.

Herr, Richard A. "A Child of the Era: Colonial Means and Ends?," *New Guinea. and Australia, the Pacific and South-East Asia* IX (July, 1974): 2–15.

Hogbin, Ian (ed.). *Anthropology in Papua New Guinea.* Melbourne: Melbourne University Press, 1973.

Hooper, Paul F. "A History of Internationalism in Hawaii Between 1900 and 1940." Ph.D. dissertation, University of Hawaii, 1972.

Howe, K. R. *Where the Waves Fall.* Honolulu: University of Hawaii Press, 1984.

Inder, Stuart. "Leaders and Their Legacies," *Pacific Islands Monthly* LVIII (December, 1987): 27.

Keith-Reid, Robert. "Regional Blocs Grow: Melanesian, Polynesian Moves Raise Spectre of Divisions," *Islands Business* (Suva), XIV (February, 1988): 8–9, 38.

Kirch, Patrick. *The Evolution of the Polynesian Chiefdoms.* Cambridge: Cambridge University Press, 1984.

Mara, Ratu Sir Kamisese. *Selected Speeches.* Suva: Government Press, 1977.

Mitrany, David. *A Working Peace System.* Chicago: Quadrangle, 1966.

Neemia, Uentabo F. *Cooperation and Conflict: Costs, Benefits and National Interests in Pacific Reoional Cooperation.* Suva: Institute of Pacific Studies, University of the South Pacific, 1986.

New Zealand, Ministry of Foreign Affairs. *Treaty Series.* Wellington: New Zealand Government.

———. *Parliamentary Debates, 1979: Supplements.* Wellington: New Zealand Government.

Olson, Mancur, Jr. *The Logic of Collective Action: Public Goods and the Theory of Groups.* New York: Schocken, 1965.

Pacific-Asian Congress of Municipalities. *Articles of Association and By-Laws.* Honolulu: Pacific-Asian Congress of Municipalities, 1971, 1973, 1977; Kuala Lumpur: 1981.

———. *Conference Proceedings: General Session,* 1974, 1975, 1977, 1979, 1981, 1984.

———. *International Cooperation for Better Government: Founders' Session, Honolulu, Hawaii, December 1–3, 1971.* Honolulu: Pacific-Asian Congress of Municipalities, 1971.

Pacific Islands Conference. *Proceedings of the "Pacific Islands Conference: Development the Pacific Way." March 26–28, 1980.* Honolulu: Pacific Islands Development Program, 1980.

———. *Proceedings of the Second Pacific Islands Conference: Development and Change.* Honolulu: Pacific Islands Development Program, 1985.

———. *Report of the Pacific Islands Conference Standing Committee.* Honolulu: Pacific Islands Development Program, irregular, 1980–.

Pacific Island Law Officers Meeting. *Report of the Meeting of Pacific Island Law Officers,* annually, 1981–.

Pacific Islands Producers' Association. *Constitution Establishing the Pacific Islands Producers' Association.* Suva: Pacific Islands Producers' Secretariat, 1971.

———. *Session of the Pacific Islands Producers' Association: Record of Proceedings.* Suva: Pacific Islands Producers' Secretariat, annually, 1971–1974.

Pacific Islands Tourism Development Council. *By-Laws of Pacific Islands Tourism Development Council.* Honolulu: Department of Regulatory Agencies, State of Hawaii, 1976.

———. *Charter of Incorporation.* Honolulu: Department of Regulatory Agencies, State of Hawaii, August 11, 1976.

———. *Minutes of the Pacific Islands Tourism Development Council, Board of Directors Meeting.* Honolulu: Department of Planning and Economic Development, State of Hawaii, irregular, 1976–1979.

Pye, Lucian W., and Verba, Sidney (eds.). *Political Culture and Political Development.* Princeton: Princeton University Press, 1965.

Regional Committee on Trade. *Agreed Record.* Suva: South Pacific Bureau for Economic Co-operation, annually, 1979–.

Schubert, James. "Toward a 'Working Peace System' in Asia: Organizational Growth and State Participation in Asian Regionalism," *International Organization* XXXII (Spring, 1978): 425–62.

Simmel, Georg. *Conflict and the Web of Group-Affiliations.* New York: Free Press, 1955.

Smith, T. R. *South Pacific Commission: An Analysis After Twenty-Five Years.* Wellington: Milburn, 1972.

South Pacific Air Transport Council. *Report of the Meeting.* Melbourne: South Pacific Health Service South Pacific Air Transport Council, annually, 1946–1978.

South Pacific Board for Educational Assessment. *Annual General Meeting of the South Pacific Board for Educational Assessment: Proceedings.* Suva: South Pacific Board for Educational Assessment, annually, 1981–.

South Pacific Forum Secretariat. *Agreed Record of the Fifth Meeting of the South Pacific Regional Shipping Council, 16–17 June 1977, Suva, Fiji.* Suva: South Pacific Forum Secretariat, 1977.

————. *Director's Report.* Suva: South Pacific Forum Secretariat, annually, 1973–.

————. *South Pacific Forum: Summary Record.* Suva: South Pacific Forum Secretariat, annually, 1971–.

————. *South Pacific Regional Civil Aviation Council: Agreed Record.* Suva: South Pacific Forum Secretariat, irregular, 1976–.

————. *South Pacific Regional Meeting on Telecommunication: Agreed Record.* Suva: South Pacific Forum Secretariat, irregular, 1973–.

————. *South Pacific Regional Shipping Council: Agreed Record.* Suva: South Pacific Forum Secretariat, irregular, 1974–.

South Pacific Commission. *Findings of the Meeting to Discuss the Report on the Possible Establishment of a South Pacific Board for Educational Co-operation: Report of Meeting, Suva, Fiji, 11 and 12 July 1978.* Noumea: South Pacific Commission, July, 1978.

————. *Report of the South Pacific Commission.* Noumea: South Pacific Commission, annually, 1947–1963.

————. *Report of the South Pacific Conference.* Noumea, annually, 1973–.

South Pacific Forum Fisheries Agency. *Report of the Meeting of the Forum Fisheries Committee.* Honiara: Forum Fisheries Secretariat, annually, 1980–.

South Pacific Health Service. *Inspector General's Report.* Suva: South Pacific Health Service, annually, 1947–1969.

————. *Minutes of the Meeting of the South Pacific Health Service.* Suva: South Pacific Health Service, annually, 1947–1969.

South Pacific Judicial Conference. *Papers,* 1972, 1975, 1977, 1979, 1982, 1984, 1987.

South Pacific Labour Ministers' Conference. *Report of the South Pacific Labour Ministers' Conference,* 1973, 1974, 1976, 1978, 1979, 1981, 1983.

Starke, Joseph G. *The ANZUS Treaty Alliance.* Melbourne: Melbourne University Press, 1965.

Tourism Council of the South Pacific. *Minutes, Meeting of the Tourism Council of the South Pacific,* annually, 1983–.

University of the South Pacific. *The Report of the Vice-Chancellor of the University of the South Pacific to the University Council.* Suva: University of the South Pacific, annually, 1970–.

Wightman, David. *Toward Economic Cooperation in Asia.* New Haven: Yale University Press, 1953.
Wyndette, Oliver. *Islands of Destiny.* Tokyo: Tuttle, 1968.

INDEX

ABOUT THE AUTHOR

MICHAEL HAAS (Ph.D., Stanford) is Professor of Political Science at the University of Hawaii at Manoa. He is the author of *International Organization, Approaches to the Study of Political Science, International Conflict, International Systems*, and *Fundamentals of Asian Regional Cooperation*. He edited the book *Korean Reunification: Alternative Pathways* published by Praeger in 1989, and is currently preparing another book entitled *The Asian Way to Peace: A Story of Regional Cooperation*, also to be published by Praeger.